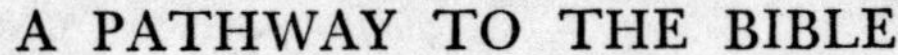

A PATHWAY TO THE BIBLE

A Pathway to the Bible

(The Old and New Testaments—
Summarized)

by SAMUEL UMEN, M. H. L., Th.D.
and
MARK B. STRICKLAND, M.A., D.D.

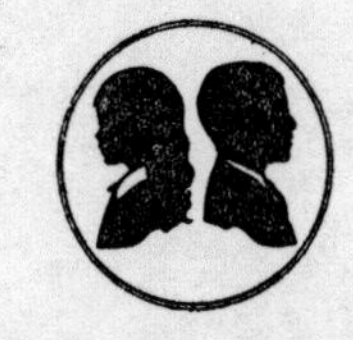

PHILOSOPHICAL LIBRARY
New York

15 East 40 Street, New York 16, N. Y.

Library of Congress Catalog Card No. 63-19258

FIRST EDITION

PRINTED IN THE UNITED STATES OF AMERICA

Dedicated

to

All Freedom Loving People

The Bible, what a book! Large and wide as the world, based on the abysses of creation, and towering aloft into the blue secrets of heaven. Sunrise and sunset, promise and fulfillment, birth and death—the whole drama of humanity—are contained in this one book. It is the Book of Books.

H. Heine

CONTENTS

PART I

PART II

PREFACE

THE BIBLE is the most venerated and most read Book in the world. Some are wont to read this Sacred Book merely as a religious exercise; others turn to it for spiritual instruction and inspiration; and, there are a few, who seek to abstract from it whatever historical information it might yield. All, however, agree that biblical literature is not the easiest to read and digest.

The Bible cannot be read intelligently and with profit, without a knowledge of its growth, development, authorship, and final acceptance as the revealed Word of God.

Mindful of this crying need, we present "A Pathway to the Bible," which not only summarizes simply and briefly both the Old and New Testaments, but also places the various writings in their proper historical setting.

It is our sincere hope that this volume may serve as a Guide to all who seek a Path to the library of the Holy Scriptures and a Lamp to illumine its Halls.

S.U. and M.B.S.

ACKNOWLEDGMENTS

We feel deeply indebted to:

. . . Reverend Placidus Riley, O.S.B., S.T.D., Dean of St. Anselm's College, who urged us to proceed with this project when it was first presented to him only as a thought.

. . . Eliza DeSchuytener, for her typing of the Old Testament part of the manuscript; Mrs. William Main and Mrs. Arthur Brand, for typing the New Testament part of the book; Rabbi William J. Leffler, M.H.L., who aided in proof reading the Old Testament section and Mrs. E. D. Hoag for proof reading the New Testament section; Alice Strickland for her patient editing and help in the final arrangement of the New Testament material.

. . . Dr. Eugene Borowitz, D.H.L., Ed. D., Professor of Education at Hebrew Union College, J.I.R.; Reverend Willis Elliott, Th.D., Ph.D.; Reverend George E. Murray, S.T.B. Ed; Reverend Ambrose W. Engel O.S.B., Professor of Theology at St. Anselm's College; and Dr. Herbert Gezork, president of Andover Newton Theological School, all for reading the Manuscript while the work was still in preparation and for their comments.

. . . Our community leaders, bankers, architects, industrialists, workers, newspaper editors, educators, clergymen, and a host of other dedicated people of every walk of life, of every faith and creed, who lovingly and enthusiastically commended the authors' efforts when they learned of this undertaking.

Above all we are thankful to: Med M. Chandler; Maxwell E. Duckoff; Walter J. Dunfey; J. Fred French; Jacob Foster II; Harold R. Goldberg; David P. Goodwin; Ralph Gottlieb; William S. Green; Frederick E. Haigis; Lester S. Harvey; Marston Heard; C. Robert Huggins; Nicholas Isaak; Faustyn K. Jaskiel; Richard Koehler; Sanford Litchman; Milton Machinist; Gordon McCown; Ralph A. McIninch; Charles S. Nims; Irwin Pariser; Leo S. Rosen; Raymond Saidel; Morris Sibulkin Jr.; Saul O Sidore; Henry R. Silver; Emile Simard; Archie Slawsby; Ezekiel S. Straw; Clifford R. Thatcher; Henry J. Turcotte and Andrew Woronka, for their wholehearted support and inspiration which made the appearance of the book possible.

S.U. and M.B.S.

PART I

B. C. E.

Before Christian Era

INTRODUCTION

The first part of *A PATHWAY TO THE BIBLE* presents several introductory chapters which offer information on how the Old Testament Books came to be regarded as holy, and how they were studied by scholars and placed in their chronological order and historical setting. This is followed by a presentation of the Books in simple everyday language.

In no instance does the writer attempt to interpret or theologize. This exercise is left entirely for the reader to pursue in the light of his own background, Faith and belief.

The author has consulted some of the best authorities on the Old Testament and has set as his paramount purpose through this part of the book to aid the average layman to read the Holy Scriptures with greater ease and a deeper understanding of the text.

S. U.

A WORD ABOUT THE OLD TESTAMENT

The Nature of the Old Testament

THE word Bible is derived from the Greek word *biblia,* which means "books." In the course of time the Bible came to be designated as the Book, the collection of the most important sacred writings of both Jews and Christians. The number of books in the Old Testament is thirty-nine or twenty-four, depending upon the reckoning of certain groups as individual books or entire units. (For example: the twelve Minor Prophets are sometimes counted as twelve separate books and sometimes as one book.)

There is no other one volume from antiquity which includes so much of human history, the history of man in the making. The Old Testament grew out of life—life such as ours—life moving on varying levels of quality, some of it sordid and some of it saintly, but all of it disclosing a movement in history, reflecting ideal, disappointment, deliverance and destiny.

The Hebrews were realists as well as idealists. If they were to know God it had to be through the experience of living. Life for them was a unity. Their God was a part of their life and they learned to know Him through the events of their life.

While the base of the Bible is history, it cannot be fully

regarded as history in a secular sense. The Old Testament is a record of world history in the realm of the soul. Man is the chief concern of the Bibleman as the counterpart of God; man in his struggle with God, who made him in His image.

The life of the Hebrew people was indeed the life of a peculiar people. They called themselves "the chosen people," chosen for a different purpose from the other great nations of antiquity. God chose the Greeks to teach the world a knowledge of beauty, and endowed them with a feeling for proportion, and with a love of symmetry, in short, with a highly developed artistic sense that fitted them to become the apostles of beauty for all humanity. Similarly, God chose the Romans to teach the world the rudiments of the science of government; and to that end gave to the Roman people a genius for law and administration. Some of us like to think that God has chosen the Anglo-Saxon people to teach the world self-government, and that it has been for that very purpose uniquely gifted with a genius for governing itself. Be that as it may, the calling and endowment of the Hebrew people was in no sense more miraculous than that of the Greek or the Roman. It differed only in the mission for which the people was chosen. God chose the Hebrew people to teach the world a knowledge of religion, and to that end bestowed upon them a genius for religion, an inherent faculty, that is, for recognizing, understanding, and expressing "the life of God in the soul of man."

Unlike their neighbors, the Assyrians, they were not a learned people. The Assyrians gave to the world the beginnings of modern science. Our knowledge of astronomy, for example, had its beginnings in Assyria, whose astrologers are said to have determined within two seconds the exact length of the solar year, and not to have been far wrong in their computation of the distances of the sun, moon and planets from the earth. Nor were the Hebrews an artistic people, like their neighbors on the south, the Egyptians. To the latter the modern world owes the beginnings of art, for the arts of sculpture and architecture flourished in Egypt more than a thousand years before the Parthenon or the Pantheon were built. The Doric column and the Roman arch were neither Greek nor Roman in origin, but Egyptian. The Hebrews, on the other hand, carved no statues; they painted no pictures; even their architecture was not their own, but was borrowed from the Phoenicians. Their first Temple was built, not by Hebrew, but by Phoenician architects. Unlike the Phoenicians, they were not a commercial people. The commercial instincts of the modern Jews are not an inherent characteristic, but have been acquired. The Phoenicians were the great traders of antiquity. The international trade of the ancient world was practically all in the hands of Phoenician merchants, and was carried on by Phoenician ships. The Hebrews were not a maritime people. They had no foreign commerce worth mentioning, except during King Solomon's reign.

Even geographically the Hebrews were seemingly least important of the great nations of antiquity. We seldom stop to think how very small the little pear-shaped country of Palestine (the "West-land") really was. It was only one hundred and forty miles from Dan to Beersheba, and only forty from the Jordan to the sea.

Yet, in spite of their being seemingly the weakest of all the great nations of antiquity, the debt of the modern world to them is immeasurably greater than that to the Assyrians, the Egyptians, and the Phoenicians combined; and it is so because their genius, though neither scientific nor artistic, nor commercial, was ethical and religious.

The religious genius of the Hebrew people found expression in their literature the so-called Old Testament.

The Importance of the Bible

Of what importance is the Bible? Why spend the time reading this ancient Book?

Apart from its religious value and authority for the synagogue and the church, the Old Testament contains the remains of a national literature which richly rewards study for its own sake. While its masterpieces may be read with pleasure and profit without regard to the age and circumstances in which they were written, they will be better appreciated as well as better understood in the light of their own times and in their places in the literature as a whole. In this literature are also the sources for the political history of the Hebrew people and for the history of its civilization and religion.

The books of the Old Testament differ widely in matter and form—history and story; legislation, civil and ritual, moral and ceremonial; prophecy and apocalypse; lyric, didactic, and dramatic poetry. The literary quality of the best in all these kinds is very high. The Song of Deborah (Judg. 5), notwithstanding the imperfect state of the text, is one of the greatest of triumphal odes; parts of Job attain the height of the sublime; some of the Psalms are worthy of a foremost place among religious lyrics; many oracles of the prophets are as noteworthy for the perfection of the expression as for the elevation of the thought; the laws are often formulated with admirable precision; in the art of narration the older historians are unsurpassed in ancient literature. These qualities appear even more conspicuous in comparison with the remains of Egyptian or of Babylonian and Assyrian writings. It is only among the Greeks that we find anything to match the finest production of the Hebrew genius. It need hardly be said that the Old Testament is not all on this high level of excellence—what literature is? But, taken as a whole, the level is surprisingly high.

Division of the Old Testament Books

Even though the books of the Bible are a collection of varied literary forms, written by many different authors, at different periods of time, yet the Old Testament with all its variety, possesses an obvious and unmistakable unity. The whole collection is unified by the fact of its being a chronicle of the religious development of the Hebrew people. It is a record of a gradually unfolding revelation, to a people divinely gifted spiritually, of God's dealings with humanity. The Old Testament, then, is characterized by variety and unity, for it is a collection of books of widely differing literary forms, brought together into one volume which is unified by the historical development that it discloses, and because of the growth of spiritual consciousness that it reveals.

Divided into three main headings, (a) Law, (b) Prophets, (c) Writings, the Old Testament serves as the basis of the Jewish religious outlook.

The Law, or Torah, comprises the Five Books of Moses, with the story of the beginning of the world, and its history till the death of the great Lawgiver.

The Torah forms the basis of Judaism, and on the principles and laws outlined therein, is built up the whole structure, which we understand by the word Judaism. The importance of the Pentateuch, therefore, cannot be overestimated. Its sanctity remains, and its influence is dominant.

"The Prophets" comprise both the historical books and the writings of the literary prophets. In the Hebrew Bible they are subdivided into (1) former, (2) latter prophets. By the former are meant such books as Joshua, Judges, Samuel and Kings; by the latter are meant the three greater prophets, Isaiah, Jeremiah, and Ezekiel, and the twelve Minor Prophets.

The third division of the Bible is "the Writings," including everything not comprised under the two former headings, viz., The Psalms, Proverbs, Job, Song of Solomon, Ruth, Lamentations, Ecclesiastes, Esther, Daniel, Ezra, Nehemiah, and the two Books of Chronicles. It should be noted that Daniel does not come to be considered among the Prophets.

Each book of the Bible aims either through story, parable, or allegory, to convey a message which would help a person better understand himself, human nature, and the world.

The Bible, with its many and varied lessons, has a place in every home and every heart among the peoples of the world. There is no finer companion than the Bible. No counsellor is better equipped to help man than the biblical lessons. The Books of the Bible are God's eternal light created to illumine man's way in his pursuit of a meaningful life.

What one reads into the Bible or out of it, depends of course upon the reader. The Bible is poetry—poetry is interpretive. Through the ages, teachers and scholars interpreted the Bible to make its poetic and symbolic language more intelligible to the layman and student.

Old Testament Language

The language of the Old Testament is almost exclusively Hebrew. The portions which form an exception are: Dan. 2:4-7:28, Ezr. 4:8-6:19 and 7:12-28 and Jer. 10:11, which are written in Aramaic. During the time of the captivity of the Jews in Babylon, their mother tongue, the Hebrew, probably fell into disuse, and the generation which grew up in captivity adopted the tongue of their captors, the Aramaic, which was then widely used among the nations. However, after their return to Jerusalem, Hebrew was still considered the sacred tongue, and the prophets who wrote after the Exile still used it. The change from Hebrew to

Aramaic was not a sudden change as far as usage is concerned, but rather a slow and gradual process. The portions of Scripture referred to above as written in Aramaic reflect the time of this gradual change.

The Hebrew language belongs to the Semitic family of languages. Its words normally consist of three consonant root letters and specific meaning is produced not merely by suffixes and endings and also to a large extent by prefixes and vowel changes within the word. Because of this, the number of word roots in the Hebrew is found to be fewer than in most Indo-European languages. "To learn" and "to teach," "to come" and "to bring," "to go" and "to lead," "to eat" and "to feed" are distinct words with us; but in Hebrew, each of these pairs has a common root, which by a form of inflection is made to convey a causative idea, and this produces what in our language would be a new word. There is a scarcity of adjectives, which however, is compensated for by the use of abstract nouns employed in a descriptive way. There are but two tenses, the imperfect and the perfect, and these do not strictly denote time, past, present or future, but rather incomplete or completed action. Apparently because of the lack of tenses and modal forms of the verb, Hebrew syntax is less exact than that of Indo-European languages, and it is more subtle and dependent on the context.

The Hebrew language consists entirely of consonants, and the vowels to be used in a word were, at first, not indicated in writing. They were supplied by the reader from his understanding of the context. Vowel points to indicate the exact pronunciation of Hebrew words originated sometime between the 5th and 10th centuries of the Common Era. It was invented by the Masoretes, (Massorettes—a term derived from the Hebrew root Masar—"to hand down"—and meaning the work of preserving the traditional text of the Bible. The men who performed this function were known as the Masoretes), in order to safeguard the exact tradition of the pronunciation, which up to that time had been transmitted orally. Two systems of vowel points were used, the "superlinear," less minute and occurring entirely above the written line of consonants and the Tiberian, adopted in Palestine and more minutely elaborated, which places the vowel points almost entirely underneath the line. The latter form is in use today.

Old Testament Style

The vocabulary of Hebrew, although very limited and only partially known, is concrete and vivid. Ideas are often expressed by objects. Thus "my horn" (Ps. 92:10) means "my power"; "Lip of Canaan" (Is. 19:18) means the Hebrew Language: "hip and thigh" (literally "leg over thigh") seems to mean utterly and completely (Judg. 15:8); religion is called "the fear of God' and morality "turning away from evil" (Job 1:1, and often elsewhere); "house" may be used for family or dynasty. The most common actions are often described visually: "he opened his mouth and spoke"; "he lifted his eyes and looked"; "he put forth his hand and took." Adjectives are rare and qualities are indicated by concrete nouns: "a man of God" means "a holy man"; "Noah was a son of five hundred years" (i.e., 500 years old); "a hill son of oil" (Is. 5:1) is a fertile hill.

Classical Hebrew is concise in structure, and impressive in uniformity: "My beloved had a vineyard on a very fruitful hill; and he digged it, and cleared it of stones, and planted it with the choicest vine; and he built a tower in the midst of it, and also hewed a vat therein" (Is. 5:1). Even political oratory, is direct and simple in ancient Israel (cf. Judg. 9:28; 2 Sam. 17:7-13).

Natural objects and phenomena are poetically endowed with soul and mind and are rhetorically personified. Job (3:9) speaks of the "eyelids of the morning" as Homer of the "rosy-fingered dawn." Deborah saw "the stars in their courses" fighting against Sisera (Judg. 5:20) and the poet of Job declares that "the morning stars sang together" (Job 38:7) when God laid the foundations of the earth; he also beheld the dawn taking hold of the ends of the earth and shaking off the wicked (Job 38:13), like a woman shaking the crumbs off a tablecloth after a meal.

The Hebrew Scriptures do not lack classical examples of straight-forward prose, sublime in their simplicity. " 'Let there be light!' And there was light," (Gen. 1:3). "For dust thou art, and unto the dust thou shalt return" (3:19). "Eye for eye, tooth for tooth" (Ex. 21:24). "Thou art the man!" (2 Sam. 12:7).

Some Biblical writers have made excellent use of irony (1 Sam. 26:15; Am. 4:4; Job 26:2-4) and sarcasm, as in two fables (Judg. 9:7-21 and 2 Kings 14:9) and in Elijah's words on Carmel (1 Kings 18:27). Proverbs (particularly chs. 25-27) is the wittiest book in the Bible: with refreshing humor the sages recognize that the most vexing type of wife is a garrulous shrew (Prov. 21:9, 19; 25:24; 27:15), while the most irritating type of husband is the indolent sluggard spending his time in bed or at home in idleness (6:9; 19:24; 22:13; 24:33; 26:13-16).

In addition to the vividness, fancifulness, sublimity and sarcasm, which have been illustrated briefly, many other moods or qualities of Hebrew style could be mentioned: pathos (Am. 5:2), exultation (Ex. 15:21), dejection (Job 3), indignation (Hos. 2:2-12) (H. 2:4-14), invective (Am. 4:1), grief (2 Sam. 18:33) (H. 19:1), tenderness (Jer. 2:2), faith (Ps. 23).

Why the Bible Is Difficult to Read

The Old Testament is not easy to read. In the first place more than two thirds of it is poetry; and for the intelligent reading of poetry a certain amount of training seems to be required to develop the artistic appreciation necessary for the enjoyment, and even for the understanding, of a literary genus devoted, not so much to the communication of ideas, as to the expression of feelings.

Biblical verse is totally different, not only from that of English poetry, but from that of any other language with which the reader of the Occident is likely to be conversant. Its constant use of symbolism, and its warmth and fervor still further differentiate if from Western poetry, either ancient or modern. Furthermore, the intelligent appreciation of the Old Testament is made immensely more difficult by its being an ancient Oriental Book. The background and the life it records is that of the ancient Semitic world, a world as far removed from ours as the East is from the West—and farther too, for between that ancient life and ours there intervene, not only the deep cleavage between the Orient and the Occident, but the long centuries that separate us from it.

THE OLD TESTAMENT CANON

The Word Canon

THE word Canon, "rule," is a Greek word believed to be derived from the Semitic word *Kaneh,* which means "measuring rod." In its relation to the books of the Bible, Canon, served as a standard—or means of evaluating the sacredness of a book before it was admitted into the Bible.

The Bible Canon is a term used to designate the whole group of books that was finally selected for inclusion into the Sacred Scriptures. The books included in the Bible are called canonical. Those books which were not included in the Bible are called non-canonical.

How the Books of the Bible Were Canonized

A logical question that occurs to the student of the Bible is: What principle governed the body of men to select only those books that are now in the Bible or canonized and not some others, which certainly must have existed at the time of selection? How did the judges know whether a book was divinely inspired? Bible scholarship has not yet determined the exact reasons for the inclusion of the books that now constitute the Sacred Scriptures or the reasons for the exclusion of the non-canonical books.

There exists a wide difference of opinion as to what made a writing canonical. There are those who hold that each writer himself knew that his book was the product of divine inspiration and, therefore, was destined to become a part of the collection of writings which were to be handed down through the generations as sacred. He claimed for his book this distinction and his claim was accepted by the people. This position is represented by W. H. Green (American Hebraist 1825-1900). "No formal declaration of their canonicity was needed to give them sanction," says Green. "They were from the first not only eagerly read by the devout but believed to be divinely obligatory. . . . Each individual book of an acknowledged prophet of Jehovah, or of any one accredited as inspired by Him to make known His will, was accepted as the word of God immediately upon appearance. . . ."

An opposite viewpoint is held by August Dillmann (German theologian 1823-1894), who says: "History knows nothing of the individual books having been designed to be sacred from their origin. . . . These books have in themselves, from the first those characteristics on account of which they were subsequently admitted into the sacred collection, but always had first to pass through a shorter or longer period of verification . . . before they were formally acknowledged . . . as divine books."

When the Canon Was Collected

When was a group or collection of writings first thought of as canonical? When did the people or their officials begin to set aside and keep distinct from other books those documents which were accepted as authoritative? We have practically no evidence which can answer these questions directly, but we have early references to the storing of archives in the sanctuary. In Ex. 40:20 the two tables of stone are described as being placed in the ark of the covenant in the tabernacle. Also in Dt. 17:18 and 31:24-26 there are references to a special place and custodians for certain sacred documents. While we are not justified in making the storing and guarding of documents in the tabernacle identical with accepting them as divine and authoritative, there is nevertheless a strong presumption that they were stored in the sacred precinct because they were considered canonical. We may thus conclude that as early as Moses' time there existed documents which were, in a sense, the Canon of that time, the Sacred Scriptures of that day.

Books came into existence containing material which readily or slowly won the approval of the religious community. Prophets, whose word was accepted as God's expressed will, either wrote down their own messages, or their followers and disciples recorded their addresses; and these became part of the accepted sacred writings. Histories were compiled, setting forth the experiences of the Chosen People in the light of their faith in God, and these came to be accepted into the Canon. It was a gradual process which seems to have been completed some time between Chronicles, the last book of the Hebrew Scriptures, and Ecclesiasticus, written by Jesus the son of Sirach (cir. 180 B.C.E.).

The Three Divisions of the Canon

The canon of the Hebrew Bible is divided into three parts. A number of scholars have attempted to prove that the three divisions of the Canon mark three steps or periods in its formation. According to this view, there was a time when the Pentateuch alone was accepted as canonical. Later, after the writings of the prophets had been tested for a longer or shorter period and approved as inspired by the Spirit of God, they too were accepted as canonical—a second Canon, as it were. And still later, after these two divisions of the Canon had become fixed and closed to other books, certain writings were found to be worthy of recognition by the religious community, and so a third Canon was formed and in turn fixed and closed, comprising the "Holy Writings."

Another theory is that as collections, one part of the Bible may have come to have a reputation as authoritative earlier than others, but the official pronouncing of them as canonical was a pronouncement that covered all three parts.

The answer to our question, therefore, as to when the Canon was collected must be that it was formed through a gradual process from the earliest beginnings of the Hebrews until shortly after Chronicles by addition of the books which the religious community from time to time came to accept as having divine authority.

THE APOCRYPHAL BOOKS AND THE OLD TESTAMENT CANON

The Term Apocrypha

THE name Apocrypha is derived from the Greek word Apocryphos—and means "hidden away." The term refers to a group of books which have been excluded from the Old Testament Canon. In Hebrew these excluded books are called "Sfarim Hitzonim"—"Outside Books"—or "Sefarim Genuzim"—"stored away books." Specifically, it refers to the fourteen books which are included in the Septuagint and Vulgate but not in the Hebrew Bible. These are the following: I and II Esdras, Tobit, Judith, the Additions to Esther, Wisdom of Solomon, Sirach (Ecclesiasticus), Baruch, Epistle of Jeremiah, the three Additions to Daniel, (the Song of the Three Holy Children, the History of Susanna, the History of the Destruction of Bel and the Dragon), the Prayer of Manasseh, and I and II Maccabees.

All the books of the Apocrypha were written by Jewish authors whose names, with the sole exception of Jesus the son of Sirach are unknown.

The fourteen books grouped under the name Apocrypha were written in the last centuries B.C.E. and the 1st cent. C.E. and were for the most part originally composed in Hebrew or Aramaic. However, II Maccabees and Wisdom of

Solomon were certainly written in Greek. All the books were probably of Palestinian origin, with the exception of Tobit, Wisdom of Solomon, and II Maccabees, products of Egypt.

Character of the Apocryphal Literature

On the whole, the books of the Apocrypha do not reach the high spiritual level of the Bible, although they contain some important Jewish conceptions, such as the praise of truth (1 Esdras), the duty of burying the dead (Tobit), the denunciation of idolatry (Baruch), the immortality of the soul (II Maccabees and Wisdom of Solomon), the honor due to the student of the law and to the physician (Sirach). It is noteworthy that prayer plays a great part in all the Apocrypha. Maccabees I has great historical value.

In fact, it was really intended by the writers of this literature to be a continuation of the Bible, inasmuch as it follows along the same lines. As it is known, the Bible consists of several divisions, law, history written with a moral purpose, prophecy, religious poetry and reflective writings. With the exception of the element of law which is scantily represented in this kind of literature, all the other elements find there adequate representation.

Why the Apocryphal Books Were Excluded from the Old Testament Canon

During the period of the Second Temple there was no fixed canon except for the Torah and the Prophets; but there were many books besides these, both in Hebrew and Greek, which could be regarded as sacred. About the 1st and 2nd centuries C.E., however, a definite canon of Hagiographa, or Holy Writings, was established. Only those books were admitted which were held to have been written before the time of Ezra when, according to tradition, the Holy Spirit ceased in Israel. The Apocrypha, being known to have been written later than Ezra's time, were not regarded as sacred; but since they contained many mentionings of the name of God (azkaroth) they could not be destroyed like ordinary books, and were therefore stored away. Accordingly, they received the somewhat euphemistic designation of *sefarim genuzim,* "books that must be stored away," "books that are to be hidden."

The Apocryphal Books in the Church

When the Christians fell heir to the Old Testament, they found in the Greek Bible which they used a number of works which were not in the Hebrew Scriptures. These "extra-canonical" books, which were a part of a vast number of Jewish writings, had been familiar to the early Jewish Christians from childhood. There was no reason in the early days of the Christian church, therefore, to ban the Apocrypha, and so the early Christians continued to read them for edification and enlightenment, and even to quote them as Holy Scripture.

Another important factor which led the early church to place the Apocrypha on the same level with the canonical books of the Old Testament, was the introduction of the book in Christian circles. In contrast with the Jewish custom of using the scroll for their sacred books, the Christians copied and distributed their Scripture in books where the Old Testament canonical books and the Apocrypha, were side by side beween the same two covers. It thus was natural for the Christians, many of whom were unfamiliar with the extent of the Hebrew canon, to treat as inspired Scripture whatever was found in their Old Testament codices.

The early church fathers treated the canonical and non-canonical books much alike. This would seem to indicate that the early Church accepted the Apocrypha as Scripture and included them in the Bible. But this was not actually the case. Origen (185-254 A.D.), who followed the practice of using the Apocrypha for instruction and edification, was enough of a Hebrew scholar to know that these books were not part of the Hebrew Bible. As a scholar, he was therefore compelled to limit the Old Testament canon to the books of the Hebrew Bible. This same problem arose in the minds of Cyril of Jerusalem (315-386 A.D.) and Jerome (347- 420 A.D.), who were more explicit in separating the Apocrypha from the canonical books. In fact, it was these two scholars who used the term "Apocrypha" for the first time to designate the books in the Greek and Latin Bibles which were over and above the Hebrew Old Testament. Jerome explicitly stated that the Old Testament Apocrypha might be read for edification, but not "for confirming the authority of Church dogmas." Yet, because of the practice of the Church, he had to include the Apocrypha, in his Latin Bible the Vulgate which became the official Roman Catholic Bible.

Augustine (354-430 A.D.), gave powerful support to the Church view by accepting the Apocrypha as canonical, although he too later admitted that there was a distinct difference between the books of the Hebrew canon and the "Outside Books" (the Apocrypha).

In the Greek Orthodox Church the Apocrypha or certain books of it, have generally been recognized as canonical.

It is clear from the above summary, that there were two opposing views of the Apocrypha, in the early Church; one which regarded these books as canonical representing the traditional view of the Church, and the other, which regarded them as uncanonical in view of the Hebrew Scriptures. These two divergent views which were never settled in the early Church, prevail today in the Roman Catholic Church, which accepts the Apocrypha as canonical, and the Protestant tradition, which does not regard these "Outside Books" as sacred Scripture.

BIBLE EXEGESIS

Jewish

BIBLE exegesis may be defined as the interpretation of the text of the Bible in order to derive from it moral teachings. The earliest Hebrew term for exegesis is Midrash, which literally means to "seek." The Bible contains snatches of history, narratives and laws. When the exegete seeks to derive a moral from a narrative, for example, the result of his interpretation is called Midrash Haggadah. When the exegete seeks to derive a deeper meaning from Biblical law, the result of his interpretation is called Midrash Halacha.

From the traditional point of view, Jewish Bible exegesis is subdivided into the four following categories:

1. Peshat (Simple Meaning), the obvious and literal meaning of text.
2. Derash, the inferred or deduced meaning of the text. This is further subdivided into interpretation for legal (Halachic) or non-legal (Haggadic) teaching.
3. Remez (Hint), philosophical or theological interpretation of the text.
4. Sod (Secret), mystical interpretation of the text.

Although there are no records to suggest exactly when academies were founded for the purpose of expounding the sacred texts, it is clear that such institutions must have started at an early period. The teachers of the Talmudic period speak of the academies as being firmly established and of great antiquity, and the very fact that all religious law had to be derived from the Bible necessitated some form of interpretation and instruction.

Hellenistic Jews (such as Philo) evolved the allegorical method which was used to adapt Judaism to Greek thought. As time progressed, we find that in the Middle Ages, further methods of Bible commentaries supplemented the old. Saadyah Gaon, faced by Moslem and Karaite criticism, broke free of the homiletic interpretation and wrote an objective commentary, utilizing contemporary secular knowledge and applying philological and independent philosophical investigation for the first time. This method developed especially in Spain; historical criticism was also evolved, and all elements were fused by Abraham Ibn Ezra. In France, Rashi relied on the literal meaning, generally having recourse to Midrash only where the text warranted; his comments were logical, clear, and based on contemporary philology. David Kimhi and Nahmanides combined the Spanish and French systems, Nahmanides, however, introduced Cabbalistic interpretation, i.e., the search for mystical symbolism behind the text, which spread with the publication of the Zohar. In the 14th cent., Jewish exegesis tended to become restricted to the more exaggerated method and declined in consequence, although Isaac Abravanel's discursive commentaries were an exception. A renascence began with Moses Mendelssohn's German Bible translation and commentary, which used the best works of the Medieval period but directed attention to secular research at the expense of tradition. Jews began to study the Bible according to Christian standards of criticism. The most recent tendency of Jewish scholars has been to relink tradition with the latest scientific and archeological deductions.

The scope of Bible exegesis is indicated by the multiple sources from which it is developed. In addition to its most finished form, that of commentaries on the text itself, exegesis is found in translations, grammatical monographs and dictionaries, philosophical treatises, and even in the works of historians. Broadly speaking, two tendencies may be observed: the dogmatic, which fosters interpretation of the Bible in accordance with and in defense of religious teaching and tradition, and the scholarly, which is based first and foremost on a careful study of the text. Both tendencies appear throughout Bible exegesis, varying in relative importance according to the temper of the age.

Christian

The history of Christian exegesis is a continual conflict between a historical interpretation of the Bible and the use of the allegorical method. The allegorical method was developed by the Stoics and applied by the Jews of Alexandria to the Old Testament, by means of which they gave profound meanings to the text, often with the utmost disregard for the plain sense of the words.

It was reserved for the theologians of Alexandria to settle the conflict—which resulted in the Church's use of two different methods—the historical and allegorical—of interpreting the Bible. These theologians, maintained the rightfulness of both but considered them, however, to repesent two separate stages. Then there was Origen's brilliant formula which stated that as a man contains body, soul, and spirit, so exegesis shows the strictly verbal, the moral and the mystical senses, challenging, supplementing and qualifying one another. This theory of the greatest Biblical scholar in the ancient church continued to dominate Christian exegesis.

Ambrose was a faithful follower of Origen; and Augustine, resembled him greatly. But it was Jerome who, under the direct influence of Rabbinical exegesis and a verbal understanding of the original, brought about the change from the method of Origen to an exegesis that fixed the verbal or grammatical sense and made interpretation historical.

With the spread of the Renaissance in the 16th cent. there came a revival of interest in ancient languages and the study of Hebrew was undertaken seriously by Christian scholars. John Reuchlin (1455-1522) wrote two Hebrew grammars and studied the Cabbala; the two Buxtorfs, Carpzov and others, issued works on Hebrew grammar and lexicography. During the 17th and 18th centuries Semitoglogists such as Edward Pocock, Albert Schultens, Job Ludolf and others helped to elucidate many parts of the Scripture through comparisons of Hebrew words with those in other Semitic languages.

Exegesis still exhibits the greatest possible differences in dealing with the text, but the principle that the meaning is to be reached by means of grammatico-historical exegesis is being more firmly established.

BIBLE CRITICISM

Bible Criticism Defined

THE popular belief among Jews and Christians has been that each book of the Bible was written as an original composition by its respective author. Bible criticism during the last two centuries has caused the old popular belief to be discarded.

In the widest sense of the term, Bible criticism is the study that seeks to elucidate all problems connected with the Bible, and thus to furnish a basis for history, theology, sociology, and other studies dealing with the times in which the Bible was written.

Bible Criticism in the Early Days

In the earlier days of Bible study, it was customary to make a distinction between "higher" and "lower" Bible criticism. The latter concerned itself solely with the text, the former with the analysis of the authorship, date and purpose of the biblical passages studied.

When the Bible was first accepted as the sacred literature of Judaism, the religious leaders of the time held it to be a compact, logical and interrelated whole. There was no scope at all for a critical interpretation. The rabbis of the

Talmudic period were fully aware of some of the difficulties and discrepancies that have become the starting points of biblical criticism; but they observed them only to explain them away, to harmonize them, because they lacked historical perspective and modern scientific method.

Bible Criticism in the 17th Century

It was not until the 17th century that the philosopher, Benedict Spinoza (1632-77), gave a decided impetus to the field of Bible study. Spinoza concluded that the first eleven books of the Bible, from the Creation Story to II Kings, formed a large, connected work of a single author. This author, presumably Ezra had combined the vast material, much of which had been composed by previous authors, but for some reason the work had never been finished, leaving the books full of inner contradictions. Richard Simon (1638-1712), a French Roman Catholic scholar, a pioneer in textual studies of the Old and New Testaments came to the same conclusion, holding the Pentateuch could not have been written by Moses, and that Ezra was apparently the editor of the material which had been compiled by earlier official historians.

Bible Criticism in the 18th and 19th Centuries

Modern Bible criticism, begins with Jean Astruc (1684-1776), a French physician who did research on the medical laws in the Bible, a professor at the University of Paris, Astruc argued in favor of Moses' authorship of the Pentateuch, but explained the discrepancies in the narrative of Genesis by supposing that Moses had drawn upon various sources in compiling the book. Finding that some of the passages use the name ELOHIM for God, while others employ the word YAHVEH (read Adonoi), he separated the book into two consistent narratives on the basis of this criterion, assigning a few other passages that did not fall into this scheme to additional documents which he supposed Moses used only occasionally. In later Bible criticism, the passages in which YAHVEH is the name of God were designated as J (following the German spelling Jahveh), and the passages in which ELOHIM is the name of God were designated as E.

Biblical scholars soon followed the lead which Astruc had discovered. In 1805, Wilhelm De Wette (1780-1849), a theologian and professor at the University of Heidelberg, made a further step in Bible criticism by pointing out the unique character of Deuteronomy, declaring that it came from a source different from the other parts of the Pentateuch. He identified Deuteronomy with the Book of the Law found in the time of Josiah, 621 B.C.E. This source Bible critics now refer to as D. Friedrich Bleek (1793-1859), a German Christian theologian, devoted his studies to the Old and New Testaments,—pointed out that the narrative of the Pentateuch had its sequel in Joshua, and that the latter book was an integral part of a group of six books which received their final form as a unit. Bible critics call these six books (the Pentateuch plus Joshua) the Hexateuch. Heinrich Georg Ewald (1830-1875), a German Orientalist, Hebraist and biblical critic, was the first to observe that J and E as indicated by Astruc continue through Exodus, Leviticus and Numbers. Herman Hupfield (1796-1866), a German Christian biblical scholar, who was professor of Old Testament exegesis at Marburg, then made the important discovery that the source E was in reality two sources, an earlier E and a later E. Accordingly, the later source, was designated as a separate source and called P.

Thus as the result of the investigations of many scholars, four different sources loomed up as the primary constituents of the text of the Hexateuch: J, E, D and P. These documents, it was thought, had been fused together by a later editor or editors who had made additions of their own to harmonize or to link together the varying source materials.

The next stage in the history of Bible criticism was to determine the chronological sequence of these four main sources. This was accomplished by Heinrich K. Graf (1815-1869), a German Old Testament scholar and Orientalist and Julius Wellhausen (1844-1917), a German theologian and Bible critic. Graf demonstrated that P indicated the latest of the literary and religious developments of the Hexateuch authors; therefore P is post-Exilic. Wellhausen placed D midway in time between J and E (about 850 to 750 B.C.E.) on the one hand and P (after 536 B.C.E.) on the other. Wellhausen thus finally, on the basis of the approximate dating of the sources, postulated a consistent development of the religion of Israel from the simple, primitive views as expressed in J and E through the concentration of the worship in the single sanctuary (in Jerusalem) in D, to the final organization, after the Exile, of fixed ritual and a hereditary priestly class, in P.

The conclusion of Graf and Wellhausen have formed practically the basis of all modern Bible criticism.

Every glory and wonder, every deep mystery and all beautiful wisdom are hidden in the Torah, sealed up in her treasures.

Moses Nahmanides

THE TORAH (PENTATEUCH)

THE first division of the Bible is called the Torah. The Greek name is Pentateuch and applies to the Five Books attributed to Moses. The Books of Moses are: Genesis, Exodus, Leviticus, Numbers and Deuteronomy. The Torah receives its title from its contents. The name itself connotes "doctrine." The Hellenistic Jews translated the term Torah as "Law." In reality, however, the Torah contains teachings as well as laws.

The contents of the Torah fall into two main parts: historical and legal. The historical portions of the Torah include the genealogy of the first Hebrew families, their settling in Canaan, their experiences in Egypt as slaves, their deliverance from bondage, their receiving of the Ten Commandments in the desert, their wandering in the desert and their eventual resettlement in the land of their fathers—Palestine.

The legal aspects of the Torah, consist of those laws which governed their ritualistic, political, economic and social life.

The Different Codes

According to tradition all the regulations found in the Pentateuch were given by Moses to Israel. Hence the Torah includes only one code. But modern Bible criticism, finds in the Pentateuch at least four different codes, ascribable to different periods and authors.

From a certain point of view the Decalogue in its various forms may be regarded as a code but is really only the rough outline of the principles underlying the earlier legislation.

The Book of the Covenant

Exodus 21-23:19 contains a code which was collected and arranged as a manual for the judge, furnishing rules to guide him in his decisions. In the wording of the superinscription —"Now these are the judgments which thou shalt set before them" (Ex. 21:1)—this section is clearly designated as a code.

The laws treated in this "Book of the Covenant," as the section is now commonly called, may be divided into two groups: (1) enactments relating to civil and criminal law (21:2,-22:16) and (2) moral, religious and ceremonial enactments (22:17-23:19). This code is primitive in nature.

The Deuteronomic Code

This code includes much of the material in the Covenant Code, as well as other matter of a religious and moral nature not found in the earlier code. It is intended for the whole nation, and not for special classes such as priests and judges. The Deuteronomic Code, on the whole, in comparison with the earlier more primitive codes, represents a great advance in religious and moral thought.

The Deuteronomic Code, despite its many innovations, cannot be considered as a new code. It represents rather a revised and improved edition of the Book of the Covenant, made in conformity with the new ideas of the time. Nevertheless, the Deuteronomic Code is not only a great reformative legal work, but it is also, in a certain sense, the first authoritative code. Under the leadership of King Josiah (2 Kings 23:3) the whole people agreed to regard the laws laid down in this code as authoritative. It is the first book of laws for the people, its predecessors being intended chiefly for judges and priest.

The Holiness Code

Compared with the Book of the Covenant, this code (Lev. 17-26), deals much more with moral and ceremonial regulations than with civil and criminal matters. The religious as well as the ethical point of view is a very advanced one. It endeavors to apply the moral principles of the Decalogue to practical legislation.

The Priestly Code

The Priestly Code includes the first part of Lev. 1-17, most of the legal sections of Numbers, some portions of Exodus and the section on circumcision in Genesis. This code is designated as "P" in full "Priestly Code," because it deals largely with ceremonial laws, laws relating to sacrifices and purity—matters over which the priests had charge.

GENESIS

GENESIS is the first Book of the Pentateuch. The name Genesis is taken from the Greek translation (Geneseos) of the Hebrew word Toledoth "generations" in Gen. 2:4, "These are the generations of the heavens and of the earth." The Hebrew name of the Book is "Bereshith," taken from the first word of the Hebrew text "Bereshith Bara Elohim," "In the beginning God created. . . ."

Genesis is not a history of the earth and man. It is Israel's account of its early beginnings and of the beginnings of life from the standpoint of religion. The writer was inspired to build his world on a three fold foundation: first, on life itself; secondly, on the people of Israel in their earliest beginnings; and, thirdly, on Israel's first contact with the world.

Contents

The Book of Genesis may be divided into four sections, corresponding to the four general cycles of stories found in the Book: (1) primeval history—the narratives concerning the origin of the world, the human race, the Flood, and the peoples of the earth prior to the call of Abraham—(1 to 11:26); (2) the stories of Abraham (11:27 to 25:18); (3) the stories of Isaac and Jacob (25:19 to 36:43); (4) the story of Joseph (37 to 50).

Purpose

The purpose of Genesis is not to serve as a text book of history or science. The purpose is to elaborate on the idea that Israel came upon the scene of history as the messenger announcing God and His truth to man.

Thus Genesis is a book whose theme is primarily and essentially religious and is based on a four fold central theme:

(a) God and mankind;
(b) God and Israel;
(c) God's selection of Abraham and his descendants for His service;
(d) God's providence.

While the book is one of universal scope and significance, it is particularistic in its central theme of Israel as the agent of the universal religious message.

Style

This book belongs among the supreme works of human literature. Genesis is great literature because of its realism and honesty. It does not evade facts. It describes life as it is, people as they are.

Genesis as it has come down to us, is made up of many strands and those who wove them had their own particular style of writing. However, while the styles of parts of Genesis vary, they represent the handiwork of men who were sensitive to beauty. There is the organ roll of the majestic account of the Creation in the opening chapter; the childlike imagination which lies back of the story of the Garden of Eden; the somber tale of Cain and Abel, and the deepening course of human sin that comes to its crisis in the Flood; lovely simplicities of limpid narrative, like the description of Rebekah at the well; never to be forgotten personalities, such as Abraham and Lot and Jacob and Esau; and at the climax the superbly sustained drama of Joseph that began in what seemed disaster and ended on a vice-regal throne.

The book is masterful in substance and particularly in its portrayal of human character such as Abraham the adventurer; Isaac the quiet man; Esau with his lusty appetites; Jacob, so strangely mixed of earthly craft and yet of stubborn would be consecration and Joseph the mighty dreamer. In even the best of them their failures and faults are portrayed as surely as their virtues.

Author

It is impossible in the strict sense of the term to speak of a particular author for the Book of Genesis. It appears to be the work of several men who are responsible for the book as it has come down to us from the past. The redactor who combined the work of the several authors of the book, has, perhaps, the best claim to its authorship.

Date

Genesis is the product of a long period of literary activity. The first commitment to writing of the legends of Israel took place around the 9th century B.C.E.

EXODUS

EXODUS is the second Book of the Pentateuch. The Hebrew name for the Book of Exodus is "Shemoth." This name is derived from the first words of the Book—(V'eleh Shemoth, shortened to Shemoth).

The Book of Exodus centers around one great experience, which gave it its name; the titanic struggle of the Hebrews as slaves in Egypt and their deliverance through the efforts of their leader Moses. Exodus is a Book whose subtitle might well be, "There is no God but Jehovah, and Moses is His prophet." Exodus could not be read with Moses left out. It is therefore supremely the Book of Moses.

The book carries on the history of Israel from the death of Joseph to the setting up of the Tabernacle by Moses' direction in the first day of the second year of the Exodus.

Contents

The Book of Exodus is the natural continuation of Genesis. Genesis describes the lives of the Fathers of the Hebrew People. Exodus tells the beginning of the People itself. It records Israel's enslavement in Egypt, and the deliverance from the House of Bondage. It describes the institution of the Passover, the Covenant of Mount Sinai, and the organization of Public Worship that was to make Israel into "a kingdom of priests and an holy nation." It recounts the murmurings and backslidings of Israel as well as the Divine guidance and instruction, vouchsafed to it; the apostasy of the Golden Calf, as well as the supreme Revelation that followed it—the revelation of the Divine Being as a "God, full of compassion and gracious, slow to anger, and plenteous in mercy and truth; keeping mercy for thousands, forgiving iniquity and transgression and sin; and who will by no means clear the guilty" (34:6-7).

Purpose

This book, by relating the story of Israel's redemption from Egyptian bondage, aims to convey the lesson to mankind that God is the God of Freedom, that Providence ever exalts righteousness and humbles iniquity and oppression.

Style

The style of the different parts of the book varies. The narrative of the opening chapters, describing the oppression, the plagues and the Exodus, is terse and graphic, while the description of the Tabernacle is dull, dry and technical. The only poetry in the book is the song that is sung by the Hebrews after the crossing of the Red Sea (Ex. 15). The close relationship between God and Israel, His "son and first-born" (4:22), is stressed, and He is usually represented as the national God. The God-conception itself varies; in one place the nobles of the children of Israel actually come into His presence (24:10); in another, Moses is told that he can not see His face and live (33:20); in still other passages He is revealed only by His voice (20:19) or through an angel (3:2). There are variations in vocabulary (both "hichbid" and "hahzik" are used to mean "harden"). The narrative is not always consistent; thus, in some places the Israelites in Egypt live apart, in Goshen (8:18), while elsewhere they live intermingled with the Egyptians (as in 3:22). The father-in-law of Moses is sometimes called Jethro (3:1), sometimes Reuel (2:18).

Author

The traditional belief is that Moses wrote the Book of Exodus. The critical view maintains that the book attained its present form through a long process of writing and revision by different hands.

Date

The book as we have it was completed about 300 B.C.E.

LEVITICUS

LEVITICUS is the third Book of the Pentateuch. The Hebrew title of the Book is "Vayikra," taken from the opening words of the Book, meaning "And he called."

Leviticus is chiefly a handbook on ritual, and since the ritual is principally associated with what is called in Hebrew (7:11) the "Levitical priesthood," the name Leviticus eminently fits the book.

The Book of Leviticus presents a marked contrast to the two preceding books of the Pentateuch. The dominant interest in this book is priestly and the contents are almost wholly legislative, not historical.

Contents

One half of the Book of Leviticus stresses the holiness of God; the other half of the book stresses the fact that if God is holy we must be holy likewise, if we are to approach Him as He should be approached.

Chapters 1-7 define the laws of sacrifice for the individual, for the congregation, and for the priests. Chapters 8-10 describe the inauguration of worship in the completed Sanctuary. Chapters 11-17 deal with the laws of clean and unclean, of purity and purification, culminating in the institution of the Day of Atonement. Chapters 18-26 legislate on marriage, personal and social ethics ("Thou shalt love thy neighbour as thyself"), the Sacred Festivals, land tenure, and conclude with a solemn exhortation on the connection between religion and national welfare. Chapter 27 is a supplementary chapter on vows and tithes.

The moral prescriptions of Leviticus were and still are of the greatest influence, stressing the holiness of the home, charity, justice, all duties to fellow men, and the sanctification of God's name (Kiddush Hashem), and liberating men from brutality and bestiality. Many Jewish virtues can be traced back to this book, which was often used for the initial acquainting of children with the Scriptures.

Purpose

If there is any purpose at all in the rigid requirements of the Law of Moses and in the elaborate sacrificial system developed in the Levitical code, it is to bring about a consciousness of sin.

Style

While the style of the book varies in parts, on the whole it may be said that aside from the value of the laws themselves, they are presented in a dry, uninspiring, stereotyped form.

Author

The Book of Leviticus, like the preceding books, is traditionally ascribed to Moses. The critical view, however, is that several hands are responsible for the form in which it has come down to us.

Date

The attempt to date the Laws of Leviticus with any precision is hopeless. Hebrew law grew by precedent, adaptation and codification. When considered in its final form, the book may be dated as post-Exilic or between 500-450 B.C.E.

NUMBERS

NUMBERS is the fourth Book of the Pentateuch. The name is derived from the Latin word NUMERI. It received this name undoubtedly from the fact that it contains the record of the two censuses, one taken at the end of the sojourn at Mt. Sinai, and the other at the beginning of the encampment on the plains of Moab.

The Hebrew title for the book is "Bamidbar," ("in the desert"). "In the desert" is perhaps the best description of the contents of the book.

Contents

The book contains laws, narratives, and poetry, which deal with Israel's experiences of forty years in the desert.

The book is a historical deposit taking up the thread of Israel's history at the point where the Book of Exodus left it.

Numbers may be divided into three divisions. The first division contains the account of the final preparations for the departure from Mt. Sinai (1:1-10:10). The second division (10:11-22:1) relates a limited number of events and the enactment of various laws which occurred on the journey through the wilderness (desert), which covered a period of about forty years. The last division (22:2-36:13) recounts incidents and enactments of laws during the encampment on the plains of Moab, and covers a period of approximately one year.

Purpose

The purpose of the book is to reveal God's redemptive activity operating in behalf of His people.

God's loving care for His people is illustrated by the institution of the sacrificial system, the establishment of the priestly and Levitical service, the laws of purification, the miraculous provisions for temporal wants in times of privation, and in the experiences of successes and reverses, all of which were predicated on the condition of faith in Jehovah.

Style

As the contents of the book vary, even so does the style change from simple narrative, to elevating poetry, to dull legalism.

Author

While traditional Judaism holds that Moses is the author of the book, modern Bible scholars maintain that the book is the result of a long historical development and the work of several hands. It is to be noted that there are statements in the Book of Numbers, which can hardly be the words of Moses. The personality characterization given in (12:3) would be impossible to interpret as a judgment by Moses upon himself.

Date

Bible critics believe that the bulk of the Book of Numbers particularly Chapters 10-12, and parts of 13 and 14 belongs to the 8th century B.C.E.

DEUTERONOMY

THE Book of Deuteronomy is the fifth book of the Pentateuch. The title Deuteronomy is derived from the Greek (deuteronominon). It is a translation of the Hebrew (Mishnah Torah = Repetition of the Law). This was the name of the book in Talmudic times. Later the name was replaced by the title of "Debarim" (words). The book begins with the expression "Eleh Hadebarim"= "These are the Words."

Contents

The book is almost wholly in the form of addresses. Moses briefly recalls the history of the wanderings of the Hebrews in the desert, impressing on every turn the lessons of their experience (Deut. 1:3).

The conception of religion which dominates the whole book, is most conspicuous in chapters (5-11). There is but one God, supreme in might and majesty, constant in purpose, faithful to His word, just but compassionate. He is not to be imaged or imagined—in the likeness of anything in heaven or on earth; idolatry, divination and sorcery are strictly forbidden. The essence of religion is love (Deut. 6:4), the love of God to his people and their responsive love to Him. In the relations of men to their fellows, whether countrymen or strangers, humanity and charity are the prime virtues.

Although a number of the laws in Deuteronomy are paralleled by similar legislation in the preceding books of the Pentateuch, there are many which are to be found only in Deuteronomy itself.

Deuteronomy is the only book of the Pentateuch that embodies any legislation on the subject of war. It provides for an exemption from service to those who are newly married, or who have just built a new house, and those who are afraid. A city that is attacked must first be summoned to surrender; fruit trees are not to be destroyed as a measure of war (20:1-20; 21:10-14). Deuteronomy is the only book of the Pentateuch that legislates on the question of divorce. Noteworthy also are its individual humanitarian and safety laws, such as the prohibition of taking a mother bird together with its eggs, and the commandment to build a parapet on every roof (22:6-8).

The Book of Deuteronomy aside from the part dealing with legislation, consists of the addresses of Moses, which are oratorical, emotional and vivid. The theology expressed is that of monotheism; there is but One God, all else are mere idols.

God stands in a special relationship to Israel; they are His people, whom He has led out of the slavery of Egypt into freedom, whom He has preserved in the desert, and to whom alone He has given His law. God chose Israel not because of its numbers or its merits, but out of sheer love (7:7-8); in turn the duty of Israel is "And thou shalt love the Lord thy God with all thy heart, and with all thy soul, and with all thy might" (6:5).

Purpose

In no other book of the Pentateuch is God's relationship to Israel and Israel's relation to God made clearer.

The chief purpose of Deuteronomy is to show that God's

nearness to and love for Israel can only be preserved by obedience to His law. There is constant reference in Deuteronomy to the law as promulgated by God for the guidance of Israel. It is not too hard for Israel to observe, nor is it far off. It is not in the heaven or beyond the seas, . . . it is rather in the mouths and the hearts of all who accept it (30:11-14).

Style

In Deuteronomy, there is flowing impressive oratory. The beauty and effectiveness of Deut. are chiefly due to the skill with which the author amplifies his thoughts, and casts them into well-balanced sentences. The importance of the subject obliges the author to expand and reiterate more than is usually the case with Hebrew writers; nevertheless, his discourse always maintains its freshness and is never monotonous. The author of Deuteronomy stands unique among the writers of the Old Testament.

Author

According to the traditional view, Deuteronomy, was written by Moses, with the exception of the last chapter, which Joshua wrote describing Moses' death. According to Bible critics the work is a composite, the earliest portions of which are held to have been written in the 7th century B.C.E.

Date

The Book of Deuteronomy represents the final result of a series of editorial expansion beginning in 621 B.C.E., and ending about 400 B.C.E.

Let us recall the tone and accents of the Prophets of Israel. It is their voice we hear when a great injustice has been done and condoned. From the depths of the centuries they raise their protest.

Henri Bergson

NEVIIM (THE PROPHETS)

THE prophets are classified as the "earlier prophets" and the "later prophets." The Books of Joshua, Judges, Samuel and Kings, fall into the category of the "earlier prophets." The books of Isaiah through Zechariah, are categorized as the "later prophets."

The prophets are also classified as "major" and "minor" prophets. This does not mean that one prophet is more important than the other but merely that the works of a "major" prophet happen to be longer.

The Word Prophet

The Hebraic word for prophet is closely allied to an Arabic word that means to proclaim something or to carry out some mandate. It would appear, therefore, that the Hebrew word in its root meaning signified the delivery of some message and that the prophet was a designated speaker. That such actually was the fundamental meaning of the word among the Hebrews appears from a passage in Exodus, where we are told that Moses hesitated and drew back from his vocation to deliver Israel, saying, "O Lord, I am not a man of words, neither heretofore, nor since thou hast spoken unto thy servant: for I am slow of speech, and of a slow tongue." And the Lord, accordingly, designated Aaron as

Moses' spokesman, saying, "And he shall be thy prophet unto the people: and it shall come to pass that he shall be to thee a mouth, and thou shalt be to him as God" (Ex. 4:10).

The prophets themselves trace their mission and message to God as the immediate source. They had a first hand awareness of a Character, a Personality, a Voice which charged them with a message.

The prophets were great teachers of moral and religious truth in its application to the people whom they addressed. The cardinal word in all their discourses was God.

The Prophets Were Not Philosophers

The prophets were not philosophers. They did not indulge in abstract discussions about God. They acted as a conscience to both rulers and people. They were God's agents in teaching of the nature of true religion.

To the prophets the thing that mattered was not so much the conception of God, as what experiences in life were regarded as manifestations of His activity, and what forms of behavior seemed consistent with the recognition of His godhood. For they realized intuitively that the conception of God or the God idea, was necessarily based upon those interests and purposes to which men attached supreme importance. Not what God is in Himself, but what He means to man, what He means to the world, was their concern. How God created the world was to the prophet a question of little importance. Neither were they particularly curious about life after death. It was the commandment of God, "Thus shalt thou live" that absorbed their attention.

The word of God and moral goodness, have thus become synonymous in prophetic speech; each has become a commandment. "For I desire mercy, and not sacrifice; and the knowledge of God more than burnt offerings." "There is no truth, nor mercy, nor knowledge of God in the land." "For they proceed from evil to evil, and they know not me, saith the Lord." "Did not thy father eat and drink and do judgment and justice, and then it was well with him? He judged the cause of the poor and needy; then it was well with him. Was not this to know me? saith the Lord." "Thus saith the Lord, let not the wise man glory in his wisdom, neither let the mighty man glory in his might, let not the rich man glory in his riches: but let him that glorieth glory in this, that he understandeth and knoweth me, that I am the Lord who exercise loving kindness, judgment and righteousness in the earth; for in these things I delight, saith the Lord." "They shall not hurt nor destroy in all my holy mountain: for the earth shall be full of the knowledge of the Lord, as the waters cover the sea."

The Prophets as Conscience to the World

The Prophets considered themselves as their brother's keeper. They were high minded patriots as well as religious zealots. They grieved at both the corruption and the afflictions of the nation. They suffered as they contemplated the ruin to which the folly and wickedness of Israel's rulers and politicians were leading their people.

The prophets were always protesting against existing conditions, against the tendency to degrade the worship of Jehovah into a sensuous ritualism, and against the mistaken policy of trying to strengthen the political life of the nation by worldly alliances with their idolatrous neighbors.

By stirring address, by the lyric utterance of impassioned poetry; now by symbolic acts, now by written tract; by whatever best means were at hand, the prophets sought to impress upon the half awakened conscience of the nation, upon careless monarchs and even more careless people—the divinely inspired truths that glowed within their own enlightened souls. Sometimes they played the role of statesman, fearlessly advocating the theory that Israel was a theocracy; sometimes they played the role of social reformers, pointing out the evils of the social system. Always they stood forth as ethical and religious leaders.

Contribution of the Prophets

The preaching of the prophets never varied in its insistence upon the idea that religion is in the first place a matter between man and His Maker, then a matter between man and society; that it must inspire men to act justly toward others, and that no people can be called religious that does not demand justice for itself and do justly to others.

As the earliest exponents of the fundamental truth that religion and ethics are inseparable, that the chief concern of religion is development of character, the equitable adjustment of human relations, and the conquest of poverty and vice; and that these concerns are the pre-requisite to a realization of the long deferred hope of the Kingdom of righteousness on the earth, the prophets made their vital contribution to society.

The ethical and religious teachings of the prophets may be summarized in three fundamental propositions:

1. To be faithful to the covenant between Jehovah and Israel, whereby Jehovah had chosen Israel out of all the nations of the earth to be His people, and whereby they in return had elected to serve Him faithfully.
2. The building up of a Kingdom of God on earth—which was to be the external expression of the covenant between Jehovah and Israel.
3. The conservation of the Hebrew state, as the condition of realizing the hope of a Kingdom of God on earth.

It is in the union of these aims both idealistic and practical that the uniqueness of Israelitish prophecy consists. A succession of men so absorbed in the "living God" and at the same time so intensely practical in their aims, at once statesmen, reformers, and idealists, cannot be found outside of Israel.

By the vigor, originality and profoundness of their moral and spiritual insights and messages, the Hebrew prophets made a significant contribution to their own nation and also to the world.

JOSHUA

THE name Joshua means "the Lord will save"—or "may the Lord save." Joshua the son of Nun was Moses' servant. He was recognized as the military leader of the Hebrews soon after their departure from Egypt. As Moses' attendant he accompanied him up the Mountain (Sinai) for the receiving of the Ten Commandments (Ex. 24:13). This fact, indicates that Joshua was a little more than a military figure. He was above all a disciple of Moses. Joshua remained faithful to Moses to the end. Thus in his last days when Moses asked that God appoint one to succeed him, God's answer was: "take thee Joshua the son of Nun, a man in whom is spirit . . . and give him a charge" (Num. 27:18).

Joshua was a man of his word, modest and simple in his wants. He did not use his position for personal aggrandizement. He was an inspiring example to his people. His example inspired faithfulness unto the Lord. "Israel served the Lord all the days of Joshua, and all the days of the elders that outlived Joshua" (24:31).

The Book of Joshua differs from the Pentateuch in the absence of legal matter. It is, however, the proper sequel to the origins of the people as related in Genesis, to the Exodus of the Israelite tribes from Egypt, and their journeyings in the wilderness. On these and also on literary grounds it is often convenient to class the first six books of the Bible as a unit under the term "Hexateuch."

Contents

The Book of Joshua falls into two main parts. The first part describes the capture of the city of Jericho and conquest of Palestine.

The second part of the book gives a detailed account of the division of the land among the tribes.

Purpose

When Jehovah established his covenant with Abraham, he made these three distinct promises respecting the patriarch and his descendants: "I will make of thee a great nation"; "unto thy seed will I give this land" (Canaan); "In thy seed shall all the nations of the earth be blessed" (Gen. 12:2,7-22:18). The first promise was measurably realized in Egypt, when the family of Jacob attained the proportions of a nation, which, at the time of the Exodus, became a free and independent people. Under the leadership of Moses, this host of emancipated slaves became an organized and disciplined nation but a nation without a home.

After the death of Moses, Jehovah spoke unto Joshua, the son of Nun, Moses' minister, saying, "Moses my servant is dead; now therefore, arise, go over this Jordan, thou and all this people, unto the land which I do give to them, even to the children of Israel" (1:2). "Be strong and of good courage; for thou shalt cause this people to inherit the land which I swore unto their fathers to give them" (1:6).

It is the purpose of the Book of Joshua to show how the second divine promise was fulfilled, and how the national expectancy, resting upon that promise, was historically realized.

Style

Joshua is written in simple prose. At the same time it does not exclude a certain amount of vigor in places where emphasis is required. Synonyms, and repetition, are employed for this purpose. "Be strong and of good courage (1:6,9). Be not affrighted, neither be thou dismayed (1:9). I will not fail thee, nor forsake thee (1:5). For then thou shalt have good success (1:8). Only be strong and very courageous, to observe to do according to all the law . . . turn not from it to the right hand or to the left" (1:7).

Verbs are piled one on another to drive home an important truth: "Only take diligent heed to do the commandment and the law . . . to love the LORD your God, and to walk in all His ways, and to keep His commandments, and to cleave unto Him, and to serve Him with all your heart and with all your soul" (22:5). "Therefore be ye very courageous . . . that ye turn not aside . . . that ye come not among these nations . . neither make mention of the name of their gods, nor cause to swear by them, neither serve them, nor worship them" (23:6). The condemnation of Achan's trespass is hammered out on the anvil of God's wrath, blow succeeding blow: "Israel hath sinned; yea, they have even transgressed My covenant . . . they have even taken of the devoted thing . . . and have also stolen, and dissembled also, and they have even put it among their own stuff" (7:10-12).

Author

The identity of the author cannot be established with certainty. There is evidence to support the view that the book was begun by an eyewitness of the events recorded therein (5:9; 6:25).

Date

The Book of Joshua was written a considerable period after the time of Joshua. It contains accounts of the death of Joshua and of subsequent events. The writing of the Book of Joshua began about 950 B.C.E. and continued until about 200 B.C.E.

JUDGES

THE Hebrew name for the Book of Judges, is "Shofetim." The word translated, means not only presiding officers in courts of law but also the heroes who delivered their tribe from oppression and then ruled until their death.

The Book of Judges continues the story of Joshua, the story of Israel's rise to nationhood. It deals with the period from the death of Joshua to the birth of Samuel.

The campaign for the Israelites' possession of their national home practically ended. They were now adjusting to an agricultural life.

The one link which bound the tribes together was their common faith in Jehovah. But this link was not secure. The culture of the Canaanites, the allurements of the nature religion of their neighbors, threatened to deprive Israel of its heritage—the covenant with Jehovah.

The period of the Judges was a time of testing, political and religious. Despite their problems, the Israelites succeeded in preserving the ideals imparted to them by their great leaders of the past, which eventually gave rise to kings and prophets who were to make their permanent mark upon the advancement of the human race.

Contents

The Book of Judges, in its present form, appears in three

unequal parts: an introduction telling of the seizure of the land by the various tribes (1:1-2:5; the main section, dealing with the actual stories of the Judges 2:6-16:31); and an appendix containing a number of stories illustrating the conditions of the times (17:1-21:25).

Purpose

The Book of Judges serves as source material for the study of the religious and historical development of Israel.

Style

The major portion of the book consists of narratives, presented in simple prose. Each of the stories centers around an important figure.

Author

There are various opinions as to when and by whom the book was composed.

Date

It is believed that the book was written in sections at different periods. Some scholars claim that the book was composed during the reign of King David between 1042 and 1023 B.C.E., and that it was edited in its present form in the 6th century B.C.E.

SAMUEL (1 and 2)

ORIGINALLY the Books of Samuel 1 and 2 were one book. The Hebrew name for Samuel is "Shemuel." The derivation of the name is by way of assonance rather than of etymology, as if "Shemuel" were a contraction of "Sha ul me'el" (asked of God).

It is difficult to account for the title of these books which bear the name of Samuel because they deal quite as much with Saul and David as with Samuel. It may be an indication of the powerful impression which the personality of this great leader made on the generations that followed, or it may be only the fact that Samuel figured so prominently in the early part of the books.

Samuel was a priest and prophet who lived in the 11th century B.C.E. The story of his life is recorded in 1 Samuel chapter 1-25. He was consecrated to the service of the shrine at Shiloh by his mother Hannah, who made a vow that she would dedicate him to God if her childlessness were removed and she gave birth to a son. When Samuel was born, Hannah, his mother, brought him to the Sanctuary as soon as he was weaned. He was then reared by the high priest Eli. There he received the call of God.

Samuel was undoubtedly one of the most important leaders of the Israelites. His spiritual encouragement and his farsightedness helped to preserve the existence of the nation.

The fact that one of the books of the Bible is named after him, although it includes events long after his death, shows how strong his influence was.

Samuel was a stern moralist; but the age required this very quality which he possessed. It was due to him that Israel did not become completely demoralized in the dark period of Philistine vassalage. It was probably as a result of his influence that there are fewer instances of lapses into idolatry in the period covered by this book than in any other age in pre-exilic Hebrew history; and it was his leadership which guided the people in the transition from anarchy to monarchy. From being a loose association of tribal units, Israel became a united nation; and the monarchy was at once the symbol and the agent of the union.

The Books of Samuel complete the history of the "Judges of Israel (11th century B.C.E.), and begin by relating the events which led to the institution of monarchy under Saul, the part played by Samuel being especially prominent (1 Samuel 1-14). The interest is then transferred to David, the founder of the Judean dynasty, and his early life is narrated with great wealth of detail. As Saul loses the divine favor, David's position advances until after the death of Saul and the overthrow of Israel. He gains the allegiance of a disorganized people (1 Samuel 15, 2 Samuel 4), and Jerusalem becomes the center of his empire (5-8)—C. 1000 B.C.E.

Contents

Roughly speaking, the books may be divided into three main sections; the first treating of Samuel (1 Samuel 1-15); the second treating of Saul (1 Samuel 16-2 Samuel 1); and the third treating of David the King (2 Samuel 2-24). These divisions are not sharply marked because Samuel holds the reins until the rejection of Saul and then immediately anoints

David. The whole of Saul's reign is, on the one hand, a sort of regency under Samuel and, on the other, a powerful conflict with David, his newly appointed successor.

Probably the most outstanding characteristic of the history recorded in these books is its powerful domination by the theocratic principle. It is a record of genuine history, but history dominated and directed by a great religious belief. Social organization, legal codes, and even the movement of armies came under the domination of the faith in Jehovah.

Purpose

What particularly the author or authors of the Books had in mind to convey through the data, is not altogether clear. As for us, the books serve to shed light on the religious ideas of the period.

Style

Samuel is written in fine Hebrew prose. The sentences are terse. The narrative is lively, and the depiction of the characters is vivid.

Author

The Books of Samuel, like almost every other Old Testament writing, are a compilation from various sources.

Date

Robert H. Pfeiffer, in his "Introduction to the Old Testament," page 362 says, "We may date 1 Samuel with some assurance about 750 B.C.E. and tentatively 1 Samuel 17 and 20, in their original form somewhere in the following century. The rest seems to belong to the century 650-550 B.C.E."

KINGS (1 and 2)

THE Hebrew name for the Books of Kings is "Melachim." The Books of Kings, like the Books of Samuel, were originally one book.

The Books of Kings continue the history of the monarchy, begun in the Books of Samuel, down to the Babylonian captivity.

The introduction of the monarchy brought a tremendous strengthening of Israel's political power and religious unity. It set forth cultural movements otherwise impossible of attainment. The pooling of all forces, causing great prosperity and general security, made room for an intelligent recording and appraising of historic events. Due to cultural progress the number of people able to read became larger, and prose writing more general.

At the royal courts men were specifically assigned to keep records of important political transactions. But still more important is the fact that Israel in those days produced a private literature.

The great Kings inspired private persons to write biographies and court histories. And, as the great Kings inspired biographies, so also must the great prophets, such as Elijah, Elisha, Isaiah, and Jeremiah, have inspired men to write about them.

Contents

The principal events in the history narrated in the Books of Kings may be summarized as follows: (1) The last days of David's reign. (2) The Glories of Solomon's reign. (3) Solomon's Apostasy, polygamy and consequent punishment, his decline and death (2:1; 11:1-43).

Purpose

The writer of the Books of Kings is interested in teaching his readers certain outstanding religious principles, but it never becomes the main object of his presentation. However, the historical records serve as the vehicle of moral and spiritual truths which are conveyed to the reader.

The account of the rise and fall of Solomon, for example, drives home in an impressive manner the lesson that so long as man walks in the path of righteousness all is well with him; but no sooner does he deviate therefrom than he becomes subject to Divine punishment. This is true of a king as well as of a common man. And, as with the individual, a people's obedience to God is rewarded by national security and prosperity while disobedience is punished by national calamity.

Style

The author is particularly effective in dialogues (18:7-15, 17; 21:2; 5-7) and description of scenes. His use of irony and sarcasm is unexcelled. His great achievement is his depiction of the gigantic figure Elijah.

Author—Unknown

Date

It is believed that the compiler completed his work before the destruction of Jerusalem in 586 B.C.E. The final chapters of the books, were added between 561 and 538 B.C.E.

ISAIAH

THE name Isaiah means "salvation of Jehovah." Isaiah was born in Jerusalem about 760 B.C.E. Isaiah was married. He had two sons, who bore symbolical names which were standing witnesses to the prophecies uttered by their father—Shear-jashub ("remnant shall turn") and Maher—Shalalhash-baz ("the spoil speedeth, the prey hasteth"), 7:3, 8:3. That Isaiah belonged to the aristocracy of Judah may be gathered from his intimacy with the chief priest Uriah (8:2), and from the ease with which at any time he could obtain access to the King. He was thoroughly familiar with life in the city of his birth. As a youngster, he walked through the vineyards and the orchards outside the city walls, and saw donkeys and oxen in their stables. In the city he noticed men clad in scarlet or crimson, street minstrels, society ladies parading with outstretched necks ogling with their eyes tripping along as they walked, and jingling with their feet. (They wore bells on their ankles.)

In religion, idolatry (2:8), formalism (1:10, 29:13) and skepticism (5:19) took the place of reverent worship and moral fellowship with God. The social life of the period was marked by injustice and bribery (1:23), by debauchery (5:2), and despotism (5:7). Political plans were not shaped by trust in Jehovah, but on the principle of proud reliance upon such human resources as a well-filled treasury, strong armaments (2:7), and alliances with other powers. The true consciousness of God had faded from the national life, and therein lay its sin. Men were blind alike to His majesty (2:11), His work (5:12). The city of Jerusalem could give itself up to festivity at a crisis when the occasion called for tears (22:1-4). The nation's attitude was one of self-conscious pride and entire forgetfulness of Jehovah.

Isaiah's call to the prophetic ministry came about 740 B.C.E. He was then about twenty years old and had grown up in a time of national peace and prosperity. The call of Isaiah in 740 B.C.E., marked the end of Israel's power and prosperity which she enjoyed for about forty years.

It fell to Isaiah's lot to prophesy in one of the most critical periods in the history of his people, when the greatest empire of the time (Assyria) was threatening its very existence.

The work of Isaiah began toward the end of the reign of King Uzziah, and extended then through the reigns of Jotham and Ahaz, and on into that of Hezekiah.

Isaiah like his predecessors Amos and Hosea, was called on to rebuke the sins of the prosperous in Judah and Jerusalem.

At that time the great empires were Assyria, whose approach to Judah was from the North, and Egypt from the South. In Ahaz's time Judah's policy was to court the aid of Assyria; in Hezekiah's time, that of Egypt. Each of these empires was ready to help, but that made Palestine the meeting place of rival powers. Isaiah's policy was that Judah should avoid all entangling alliances and put her trust in God. This was a time of turmoil from without and conflicting policies from within, which is reflected in many of the prophecies of Isaiah.

Isaiah devoted all the powers of his mind, all his spiritual strength, even the incidents of his private life, to the performance of his mission, endeavouring to lead his countrymen in the ways of God and to impose the Divine will upon the conduct of the state, its rulers and its citizens. Isaiah was a vigorous thinker, with a clear and acute mind, and a rare faculty of imagination. To his power of thought he added strength of will and a high courage. Before king or people he was fearless and resolute. In his single person were united the fervid orator, the statesman, and the wise moralist. Altogether he must be ranked as one of Israel's greatest men. Politically and religiously, Isaiah was the foremost figure in Judea during a period of exceptional stress and change, and he is justly reckoned "by far the most sublime of the three greater prophets" (Herder).

Message

Isaiah makes faith the basis of political as well as religious life. He declares that upon the presence and absence of faith in king and subjects depends the existence of Judah as a Kingdom: "If ye will not believe ye shall not be established" (7:9). He insists upon faith as the determining factor in human destiny, and the true source of strength: "He that believeth shall not make haste" (28:16). That the prophet himself as well as his disciples exercised such faith is clear from his attitude in a day of darkness: "I will wait upon Jehovah that hideth His face from the house of Jacob, and I will hope in Him" (8:17). All who dissociate themselves from the national unbelief shall find salvation: "The remnant of Israel shall stay upon Jehovah, the Holy One of Israel, in truth" (10:20).

He is strong in the conviction that of the faithless nation at least "a remnant shall turn to the Lord" (1:27, 4:2, 10:21). For giving itself up to sin the nation must be punished, but as the depository of revelation it cannot be utterly destroyed. The righteous of Zion and her converts ("those in her who turn") shall survive the judgment, and from this imperishable "holy seed" shall spring the ideal "Israel of God." From Zion as the earthly seat of Jehovah's rule, light and peace shall emanate to all nations (2:2) and the poor among men shall rejoice in the Holy One of Israel (29:18). The radiance of great light shall transfigure the land. The nations shall place themselves voluntarily under the sway of Jehovah, and war shall cease (2:3).

Isaiah's Messianic predictions embody the ideal of the Kingdom of God on earth and the eternal greatness of Zion. He prophesied the advent of a time when nations "shall beat their swords into plowshares and their spears into pruning-hooks," when "nation shall not lift up sword against nation, neither shall they learn war any more" (2:4-5). He looked forward to the era when "the wolf shall dwell with the lamb, the leopard lie down with the kid," the infant "play on the hole of the asp," and the calf and the young lion together be led by a child. And the world "shall be full of the knowledge of the Lord as the waters cover the sea" (11:6-9).

Isaiah is rightly described as "the prophet of faith." In words of fire he sought to impress this faith upon his generation, and to convince them that the Divine government of the world was based on morality, justice and equity.

Style

The book of Isaiah takes rank as one of the finest compositions in the Hebrew tongue. By whatever standard judged, it possesses high literary merit. In elevation and beauty of thought, in imaginative power, in vividness of word painting, it bears the stamp of true poetic genius. The language, dignified yet natural, terse yet rhythmical, pictorial yet pointed, reveals the hand of the literary artist. "There is astonishing directness and sureness of touch in his phrase, as one who knows when he has hit the mark, and does not need to strike a second time" (Skinner). Isaiah, "has a strength and power of language, a majesty and sublimity of expression, an inexhaustible richness of fitting and stirring imagery, that overwhelms the reader, nay, fairly bewilders him" (Cormill-Prophets of Israel, P. 68).

Date

The Book of Isaiah is a great collection of prophecies of various ages from the middle of the 8th century down perhaps to the third, with some minor additions of even a later date. The book as we have it is believed to have appeared about 200 B.C.E.

Deutero (Second) Isaiah

The last twenty-seven chapters of Isaiah differ from the first thirty-nine in historical perspective, literary style and religious thought. As a matter of fact some of the oracles in chapters 40-66 seem to belong to an age much later than that of the prophet Isaiah. The whole of chapters 40-66 or at least the section of 40-55, which has come to be known as Deutero (Second) Isaiah, points to the time of the Exile, a century and a half removed from the period of the prophet.

Although the tradition that the whole book 1-66 was written by Isaiah, the son of Amoz, who lived and prophesied in Jerusalem during the latter half of the 8th century B.C.E., was all but universally accepted throughout the centuries prior to the rise of modern biblical scholarship, the theory that chapters 40-66 originated in the time of the Exile, came to be regarded favorably by Old Testament scholars in increasing numbers in spite of persistent opposition.

In no passage do the chapters under consideration indicate who the author was. We know nothing of the man whom we call "Second Isaiah" except what we may infer from his words addressed to Israel. Of himself he says little if anything. We are told neither his name, his parentage, his home, his status, his age, whether he was married and had family, nor a single incident out of his experience. He remains for us—to use a word of his that he employed with a different meaning—a voice. But from that voice we can gather much regarding him who uttered it. And first we can perceive the conditions which prevailed about him. "Comfort ye, comfort ye my people" he begins; and that at once gives us the setting. For the Israelites of his day needed comfort. They were a broken and despairing people.

What made them so? Unquestionably it was the fall of their national state and especially of Jerusalem with its Temple. The fatal year 586 B.C. marked a change in the temper of the Hebrew people. Before that it was only the prophets who had talked of ruin; the majority continued stout-hearted, hoping in spite of repeated disasters that the tide would yet turn in their favor. After 586 B.C.E. it was the prophets who hoped, while those about them were plunged in despondency.

The land of Palestine, or at least the former Kingdom of Judah, lay very largely in ruins. Second Isaiah speaks of the "desolate cities" (54:3), "the desolate heritages" (49:8); "the waste and desolate places, the land that hath been destroyed" (49:19). Jerusalem was "heaps," and as for the Temple its foundation must be relaid if it was ever to rise again (44:28). The people also were terribly diminished in number and strength. He calls Zion a widow bereaved of her children (49:19) or a barren mother without off-spring (54:1).

Wherever he turned he saw his people plunged in wretchedness. The chief hardship was exile itself: they were not "let go free" (45:13). But there was more than that. Second Isaiah makes Jehovah accuse Babylon of pitilessness:

"I gave them into thy hand: thou didst show them no mercy;
Upon the aged has thou very heavily laid thy yoke" (47:6).

He says again:

"This is a people robbed and plundered, they are all of them snared in holes,
And are hid in prison houses:
They are for a prey, and none delivereth; for a spoil, and none saith, Restore" (42:22).

The Jews lived in constant dread of violence and even death. They "feared continually all the day because of the fury of the oppressor, as though he made ready to destroy" (51:13).

One of the hardest things they had to bear was widespread contempt. They were nobodies, their nation dragged in the dust. Insults came from every quarter. They dreaded not only blows but taunts; they "feared the reproach of men, and were dismayed at their revilings" (51:7). Jacob was a "worm" (41:14).

The effect of all this upon the mind of Israel had been unhappy. Instead of bringing out their courage and their faith in God it had done just the reverse. We have already seen how they lived in apprehension; and fear has a devastating influence upon the character. They had also turned against God. Had he not cast them off? "My way is hid from Yahweh," Israel said, "and the justice due me is passed away from my God" (40:27). "Yahweh hath forsaken me, and the Lord hath forgotten me" (49:14). He had divorced their mother (Israel) and had sold them to his creditors (50:1). Some were declaring that Jehovah was played out; He had become faint and weary (40:28). His arm was shorter than it used to be; His ancient power to deliver had not proven equal to the new time with its greater needs (50:2). Some were openly defiant, angrily (45:24) taking Him to task for His conduct towards Israel (45:9) and stoutly disobeying His laws (46:12), making their obstinate neck as an iron sinew, and their brows brass (48:4). Such was the time in which our prophet found himself.

Faced with this dejected mental attitude, the Second Isaiah was spurred to action. Being a thinker and a poet rather than a prophet, he composed a spiritual epic which not only inflamed the faith of Israel, but surpassed all other writings of the Old Testament, not excepting the Books of Job and Daniel in its influence on mankind.

Though aware of his people's mental blindness and deafness, the author was deeply touched by their misery. He did not castigate them, as the earlier prophets had, but with great warmth, sympathy and tenderness, he exclaimed, "Comfort ye, Comfort ye my people, saith your God." He dispelled doubts with moving appeals, and alluring hopes, and with impassioned oratory.

To question God's power and wisdom was beyond his comprehension. Equally absurd was the thought that the Almighty Creator of the world had forgotten Israel. But the unhappy situation of the Jews, particularly in Judea, seemed to indicate that Jehovah was either indifferent or hostile to them; in the second place, the doctrine that Jehovah was the God of all nations was not easily reconciled with the old notion that Jehovah was partial to Israel; and in the third place, one could wonder if Israel was sufficiently righteous to be redeemed. The second Isaiah attempts an answer in a message—which he addresses not to Israel alone but to all mankind.

Message

Jehovah has poured out his anger on the Israelites because they were not obedient to His Law. He (Jehovah) refrained from destroying them completely because He is loyal, merciful, and intolerant of rivalry or aspersions on His honor.

Jehovah has chosen Israel as his people having given His pledge to Israel, He will keep it eternally. "For the mountains will be removed . . . but my loyalty will not be removed from thee" (54:10).

Jehovah cannot permit the heathen to destroy His people lest their gods be deemed superior to Himself. Jehovah's character thus requires the restoration of Israel; His purpose—the manifestation of His glory to the Gentiles and their conversion to His religion—demands it in the immediate future.

The divine work of salvation embracing both Jews and Gentiles has been initiated. God has chosen Cyrus the Persian to crush Babylon and to deliver Israel; having become a worshiper of the true God, he will spread His religion to the ends of the world.

Even more than Cyrus, Israel is the instrument for the conversion of the Gentiles. Israel has God's law in its heart; so Israel is the witness, the messenger, and the suffering Servant of the Lord.

No one contributed more than the Second Isaiah to transform the national religion of Israel into a religion for all men. He looked forward to the day when all men would worship Jehovah, the only true God.

Style

The style of the Second Isaiah is highly individualistic. He is fond of figures of speech. He personifies cities and Nature. The dominant note in chapters 40-55 is deep enthusiasm, triumphant joy and the inexpressible pathos of the Servant's vicarious suffering. His imagination is so vivid that on the one hand it robs him of a clear perception of reality and, on the other, creates a world of fancy more actual to him than his surroundings. The glorious redemption of Israel blinds him to his actual environment. The redeemed Israelites, he depicts marching to Zion over a fantastic highway, across a desert which is miraculously changed into a garden of Eden. The chapters of Deutero Isaiah are a succession of enthusiastic shouts, his thoughts are poured out "glowing and fluid, like molten metal."

Date

The date for the chapters of Deutero Isaiah is about 200 B.C.E.

The Third (Trito) Isaiah

Bible scholars are of the opinion that chapters 56 to 66 are the works of a third Isaiah.

The picture drawn of the third Isaiah in chapters 56-66 is one who is less spiritual, cosmopolitan and idealistic, than the Second Isaiah. The Third Isaiah appears to concern himself more with the externals of religion; nationalism and legalism.

Chapter 56:1-8 emphasizes the ordinances of religion. Chapters 56:9-57:13 are a scathing invective against corrupt religious leaders (56:9-57:2) and licentious nature worship (57:3-13). In chapters 63:7-64:12 we find one of the most moving passages in the Old Testament. It is a community lament, in which appeal is made to Jehovah's steadfast love manifested in the past history of his people.

Message

The Holy City (Jerusalem) shall be mistress of the nations; foreigners will rebuild her walls, and their kings be her servants. The material and moral prosperity of Zion will be without precedent (chapt. 60).

Style

There are passages in Trito Isaiah which rise to be the very heights of prophecy, such as 57:15-16; 58:6-14; 61:8; 64:8; 66:1-2.

The prophecy as a whole gives us a valuable insight into the conditions and religious life of Israel in the decades following 538 B.C.E.

Author

It is conjectured that Trito—Isaiah is from a number of authors who were in the tradition of Deutero Isaiah.

Date

The favored date for the chapters ascribed to Trito Isaiah is 516 B.C.E.

JEREMIAH

JEREMIAH ("Jehovah hurls") was born at Anathoth, a village four miles north of Jerusalem. The son of one Hilkiah, a priest, he appears to have lived in easy circumstances (32:6), and to have been carefully educated in all the sacred lore of Israel. He expressly acknowledges how much he owed to his parents (1:5). From (16:2) it may be concluded that he was never married.

The life of Jeremiah falls in one of the most striking and critical periods in the history of the ancient world. His ministry began in the year 626 B.C.E., the year of the death of Ashur bani-pal, the last of the great Kings of Assyria, at a time when all western Asia was being laid desolate by the inroads of hordes of northern barbarians known to the Greeks as Scythians. He witnessed the complete overthrow of Assyria culminating in the destruction of Nineveh in 612 B.C.E., followed by a decisive defeat of Egypt's last attempt at world empire in the battle of Carchemish (605 B.C.E.).

Startling events took place in his own land also. In his youth (639) a king was assassinated. Judah became a vassal of Egypt and of Babylonia, and rebelling against the latter in 597, suffered invasion, siege, and the deportation of her young King Jehoiakim and the best of her people.

When Jeremiah was called to prophesy in 626 B.C.E.,

he was not quite twenty years of age. While at first he appears to be timid, introspective, sensitive and distrustful of his abilities, tormented by fear, he soon becomes through a power which to him was divine, "a fortified city, an iron pillar and walls of brass."

His personality impresses us as that of a single-hearted prophet who boldly declared before king and people, without fear or favor, the word of Jehovah as revealed to him, and whose chief desire was to bring the men of Judah into a right relation towards their covenant God.

Jeremiah taught that a bond exists between God and Israel. This bond is in the form of a covenant—an agreement whereby God has chosen Israel as His people in consideration of the latter's acceptance of Him in a peculiar sense as their deity. He reminds Israel, of this relationship. In a beautiful simile to which he often returns, Israel is depicted as God's "bride," consecrated to Him: "Go and cry in the ears of Jerusalem, saying: Thus saith the Lord: I remember for thee the affection of thy youth, the love of thine espousals; how thou wentest after Me in the wilderness, in a land that was not sown. Israel is the Lord's hallowed portion, His first-fruits of the increase; all that devour him shall be held guilty. Evil shall come upon them, saith the Lord." (2:2).

The duties of the covenant, involved refraining from the abominations of idolatry (22:9) and observing God's Laws, Statutes and Judgments. However, the covenant, did not confer immunity. On the contrary, Jeremiah repeatedly stressed that because they enjoyed God's favor they will be punished in the event of disobedience. This is a cardinal feature of Jeremiah's teaching; hence his book abounds in predictions of calamity. This view, aroused strong and bitter resentment. For the very thing which the people relied upon was held up as the very cause of their downfall.

Early in the reign of Jehoiakim, Jeremiah appeared in

the precincts of the Temple and warned the people not to be misled by the false hope and belief that God would save the Holy City and Temple from destruction for, Jeremiah knew that it had become an article of faith with the Jews that Jerusalem was inviolable. Thus he cries out in the name of God:

"Amend your ways and your doings,
Then I will cause you to dwell in this place.
But trust not in lying words, saying,
'The Temple of God, the Temple of
God, the Temple of God' "

(*Jer.* 7:3-4)

Priests, prophets, and people clamored with one voice for the blasphemer's death, but he hurled back at them a reiteration of his warning. The intervention of some of the magnates saved his life.

Under these circumstances Jeremiah took another way of reaching the public (see Jer. 36). He dictated to Baruch (his secretary) the prophecies which he had uttered from the beginning of his mission to that time, and sent Baruch to read the roll in the Temple at the fast in the ninth month in the fifth year of Jehoiakim (603 B.C.E.). Some of the nobles had Baruch give them a private reading, and then carried the book to the king, first giving Baruch the friendly advice to put himself and Jeremiah out of harm's way. The king, as he read the roll, cut off the pages and burned them on the brazier in his chamber. Jeremiah thereupon dictated to the faithful Baruch another roll containing all the prophecies that were in the first, "and there were added besides unto them many like words." We may be sure that the second edition would have been even less agreeable reading to Jehoiakim than the first. One of the additional words is indeed preserved in Jer. 36:29-31. The chapter is of peculiar interest, because it is an account—the only one in the Old

Testament—of the origin of a prophetic book. We see the prophet reproducing, doubtless from memory, the content of oracles uttered in the course of the preceding twenty years or more and enlarging the collection for a second edition.

Jeremiah's was a sad and pathetic ministry. It was in reality a prolonged martyrdom. Alone in Judah he had to withstand idolatry and immorality, the specious self-deception produced by the fanatical idea of the Jews that in all circumstances they could rely upon Jehovah's protection. He was insulted by opposing such beliefs, he was insulted by the Temple priests, by King Jehoiakim (30:23), and by his fellow townsmen of Anathoth (11:19). Even his own kinsmen turned against him (7:6). The people generally shut their ears against his preaching. Under the burden of grief he breaks out at times into despairing woe (9:2), rash charges against the Almighty.

Small wonder, that at times he bewails his fate. Weary of the strife, he yearned for a lodge in the wilderness (9:2) cursed the day of his birth (20:14), wished that he had never become a prophet (20:7) and resolved to abandon his office.

Despite his setbacks and moments of depression, Jeremiah continued battling in the name of Him who called him to His service. If the people discouraged him, God's word comforted and strengthened him.

He was convinced that if each individual Israelite could experience God as he did, then his battle would be won. Jeremiah was the first of the prophets who sought to impart the lesson that God must be the concern not of the community alone but each individual person.

It may be truthfully said that personal religion, as it is generally understood—the quest of the individual soul for a direct experience of God's love—begins with Jeremiah. "But Thou, O Lord," he exclaims, "knowest me, Thou seest me, and triest my heart toward Thee" (12:3). Again, "Thy words were unto me a joy and the rejoicing of my heart; because Thy name was called on me, O Lord, God of Hosts" (15:16).

Message

Jeremiah's teaching is characterized by certain new and distinctive features of its own. According to Jeremiah, religion is essentially and purely spiritual. Religion is innate in man. Even the false religion of the heathen shows this. Their deities do not really exist; they are simply the creations of their own imagination (10:15, 16:9). Yet their perverted worship is a testimony to the yearning of the human spirit after the divine. Not only so; their sincere homage to their false gods renders them more acceptable in the sight of the true God than those who have the knowledge of Him but neglect His service. It was the sin of Judah that she valued worldly wisdom, physical strength, and material wealth, far above the right understanding and knowledge of Him who exercises loving kindness, judgment, and righteousness in the earth (9:23). And the iniquity of such an attitude was increased by the fact that it ran counter to what is a natural instinct in man. "Yea, the stork in the heaven knoweth her appointed times; and the turtle, the crane, and the swallow observe the time of their coming; but my people know not the judgment of the Lord" (8:7).

Style

The writings of Jeremiah are characterized by great ideas rather than by literary excellence. Although frequently powerful and searching, and not without a certain charm, the style is on the whole unadorned. There is no attempt at artistic word-painting. There is much repetition of phrases and even of whole verses (cf. 5:9 with 9:8, 6:13, with 8:10 etc.). It was perhaps natural that the prophecies of Jeremiah should in this way reflect the condition of his nation. "How could he soar, when there was so much to depress his imagination? He at any rate can touch the heart, and is free from affectation" (Cheyne: Jer: His life and Times P. 203).

Date

Although Jeremiah began to prophesy in 626, he did not commit his words to writing until he dictated them to Baruch his secretary late in 605 B.C.E.

EZEKIEL

EZEKIEL ("God strengthen") the son of Buzi, had been a priest in Jerusalem. While still young he was carried away to Babylonia in the First Captivity in 597 B.C.E. He was married and lived among the Jewish exiles in a village called Tel-Aviv "by the river of Chebar" somewhere in the neighborhood of Babylon.

Ezekiel received the call to take up his prophetic career around 593-2 B.C.E. "The heavens opened and I saw visions of God." So begins the prophet's account of the vision by which he was called to the prophetic ministry (Ch. 1). Jehovah has left his polluted and doomed Temple in Jerusalem and has gone to heaven; he would return to occupy a new sanctuary in the midst of a reborn Israel. The grandiose imagery stresses the majestic transcendence, the cosmic power, and the unapproachable holiness of the deity. The vision is followed by the divine commission to go and preach a message of "lamentations, moanings, and woe" to the rebellious "house of Israel," meaning the Judeans in Jerusalem.

At the time of his call, Ezekiel was perhaps twenty or thirty years old, having been born between 623 and 613 B.C.E.

Ezekiel was called to prophesy at a crucial time in his nation's history. In that year a plot against the domination of the Babylonian invader was being prepared by the patriots in Jerusalem and the exiles in Babylon. Ezekiel saw in this a threat to the nation's existence. He exhorted his fellow Jews against such a policy and plan.

After the fall of Jerusalem (586 B.C.E.), the prophet turned his attention to the task of comforting and sustaining the exiles in their trials of awakening in their hearts the hope of restoration, and of pointing out to them the way of recovery. Furthermore, he endeavored to equip them with moral ideals and ceremonial patterns adequate for life and service in the future kingdom which he envisioned. While describing the outward, ritualistic forms which were to be regulative in the new Israel, he set forth also the principle of individual responsibility, the necessity of a new heart, and the demands of social justice. Because of his outstanding influence upon the later cultus, he has been called "the father of Judaism."

Probably because of his priestly descent, his fellow exiles treated him with respect. In fact, his house seems to have been a gathering place for the exiles and a meeting place for the "elders" of the community (8:1, 14:1), where they came to seek him or to which they were called for conference by the prophet.

Unlike any of his predecessors Ezekiel was of the people, and not aloof from them. He was their "shepherd" and "watchman" and, in a sense the personal minister to their needs and problems.

Ezekiel found himself confronted with the necessity of providing his people with a means by which they could see hope in the very visitation of God's wrath upon them. He had to provide an answer to the question raised by the people (33:10), "Our transgressions and our sins are upon us, and we pine away in them; how then can we live?" The despair of the people was based on the conception commonly held that succeeding generations were punished for the sins of the fathers (Ex. 20:5). Ezekiel declared, that this principle is false. The present generation is punished for its own sins (ch. 8 and 17). The life of every individual has its own significance. The doctrine of individual responsibility became the basic doctrine of morality in Judaism.

A very versatile man, Ezekiel employed a variety of devices and methods with which to make known the lofty truths revealed to him. At times he dramatized his doctrines before audiences of exiles; on other occasions he resorted to the power of the pen in order to insure for his message a wider and more permanent influence. But whatever the capacity in which he served, whether as prophet or pastor, dramatist or writer, he exhibited unique qualities of mind and spirit. So skillful was he in the portrayal of truth that it is not always possible to distinguish between scenes publicly enacted and those that may be purely literary. By means of visions, symbolical acts, allegories, apocalyptic devices, dirges and oracles, he set forth the principles which he wished to convey. With the art of an Aeschylus and the skill of a Shakespeare, he has woven his variegated materials into an orderly whole, making his prophecy, regardless of the numerous alterations which have been made in the text, one of the masterpieces of the world's literature. But as for himself, it was not a work of art merely that he was preparing; it was a message of revealed truth which came to him through deep reflection and exalted experience and which called for the best literary expression that he could command. However large or small the contributions of later hands to its present form and content, the book stands as a monument to his prophetic gifts.

Message

In chapters 18 and 23 the prophet deals at length with the doctrine of individual responsibility and moral freedom.

His fellow-exiles who apparently considered themselves better than their fathers, complained that they were being punished for the sins of their ancestors. His reply was that no man is punished for the wrongs done by others. No man is tied even by his own past. The moment he ceases to be what he has been, whether bad or good, that moment God's attitude and treatment changes toward him.

"If the wicked turn from all his sins that he hath committed, and keep all my statutes, and do that which is lawful and right, he shall surely live, he shall not die. None of his transgressions that he hath committed shall be remembered against him: in his righteousness that he hath done he shall live. 'Have I any pleasure in the death of the wicked? saith the Lord Yaveh; and not rather that he should return from his way, and live' " (18:21).

Another part of Ezekiel's message deals with the restoration of Israel. In ecstasy Ezekiel saw a valley filled with dry bones. This to him was a symbol of Israel's return. Jehovah will bring the "whole house of Israel" out of its grave in the Exile and lead it back to its land. Judah and Israel will thus be united again under one king.

Ezekiel's vision of Israel living again in its land and worshiping Jehovah is a program for the future community. It is a program for the age when all the twelve tribes gathered together from Exile and Dispersion shall occupy the holy land, with a new division of the territory, with a new plan for the city of Jerusalem, a new constitution for the State, a new Temple after the old model, a reorganized ministry of religion, and a reformed worship. The main idea which runs through all this is to make impossible those sins against God, His land, His House, His people, which had been the cause of former ruin (Chapters 40-48).

Style

The poetic sections of Ezekiel's book are practically all

allegorical. His allegories are descriptive, dramatic and imaginative. The prose parts of the book are fairly lucid but not without monotony and repetition. Ezekiel excels in description, whether the scene be real or imaginary.

Date

Critics differ in opinion as to when the Book of Ezekiel was put together in complete and final form. Some believe that Ezekiel himself arranged the oracles as given in the book, others claim that they were put together at a time after the life of Ezekiel. The general date for the book is the first half of the sixth century B.C.E.

HOSEA

HOSEA ("salvation"), the son of Beeri, prophesied in ancient Israel during the period extending from approximately 760 to 735 B.C.E.

Early in his career, Hosea had discerned beneath the placid surface of the national life, the ravages which had been wrought in the religious and moral life of the people when they adopted the cult of Baal as the mode of worship of their ancestral deity. He also recognized the increasing power of a new class of wealthy landowners and traders, and the corrupt priestly and governing classes whose predatory practices resulted in the social injustices of his time. Amos' reaction to all this is summed up thusly in (chapter 4:1) of his book: "There is no truth, nor charity, nor knowledge of God (religion) in the land; naught but swearing and breaking faith and murder and theft and adultery."

To Hosea's warning that the day of retribution was at hand, the people retorted that the prophet was a fool and a madman (9:7). Hosea depicted their guilt and announced their punishment only to see them again and again plunge deeper into their infidelity.

According to Hosea, corruption pervades every aspect of life because the people have no true conception of the real nature of God, or of His desires for men. To Hosea, God is a moral Being who desires "mercy and not sacrifice, and the knowledge of God rather than burnt offerings" (6:6). This concept was at total variance with the common conception of the day, in which the god was conceived of as the lord (Baal) or husband (ish) of the land which, in turn, was conceived as the mother of its inhabitants, who regarded themselves as children of the deity. The deity was thought of as "the husband of the worshipping nationality or motherland."

While Hosea did not reject this conception, he went beyond it, lifting "the conception of the marriage relation of God and people out of the nature-sphere to which it originally belonged, into the moral sphere, and gives it developments of surprising depth and tenderness."

It was through his domestic trials that Hosea reached the consciousness of his prophetic calling. Hosea had married a certain Gomer who proved unfaithful to him. Gomer bore him a son, whom he named Jezreel, by which he intended the son to be a "walking sermon." Later, Gomer bore Hosea a daughter, whom the prophet, perhaps aware of Gomer's unfaithfulness, called "Lo-ruhamah" ("not loved"). A third child, a son he named "Lo-ammi" ("not my kin"), as if certain that he was not the child's father. In the course of time, Gomer either left Hosea or was driven from his house. She became a harlot, or, at last she sank so low as to be sold for a slave. The prophet's love still went out to her and in the open market place he bought her back, and took her once more to his house. She was put upon a strict probation, in the hope that sincere repentance might make it possible for her to be reinstalled in her former position.

This bitter experience taught Hosea the true relation of Jehovah and Israel. While Jehovah had been as a loving husband, to the Israelites, in their idolatrous worship, they behaved like a faithless wife. Yet, He yearned to win them back with a yearning still greater than the prophet's own to reclaim the guilty and thankless Gomer.

Hosea's suffering made him sympathetic with erring men, although he still held to his high ideals. And thus he adds to the picture of the true God the warm, glowing colors of a sympathetic, yearning love that welcomes the sinner the moment he turns his face toward the right and that sends healing influences to repair the damage man has wrought.

Message

Hosea's message is that God is love. As Hosea's love for his wife would not allow him to abandon her to her fate, and as he made unwearied efforts to reclaim her from her evil ways, so did the ultimate guarantee of salvation for the blinded and foolish nation lie in the character of the love that cannot tear itself away from the beloved object. This is expressed in a wealth of beautiful imagery, with which Hosea brings his book to a close. "I will be as the dew unto Israel and he shall grow as the lily, and cast forth his roots as Lebanon" (14:5).

Hosea is one of the greatest of the prophets. No other contributed so much to deepen and spiritualize the conception of religion.

Style

The writings of Hosea have a power and a pathos all their own. There are frequent plays upon words, as well as metaphors, which though suggestive, are seldom drawn out. The language is difficult and suffused with passion and emotion.

Date

The date of Hosea's prophecies is recorded in the heading of the book. Hosea prophesied during the period of (750-735 B.C.E.).

JOEL

THE Name Joel means "Jehovah is God." The name of Joel's father was Pethuel, which means "persuaded of God." THE WORD OF JEHOVAH THAT CAME TO JOEL THE SON OF PETHUEL. These names, together with the fact that God called him to the work of prophecy, would indicate that Joel was the scion of one of the many great Hebrew families whose chief delight was in the worship of their God. The date for Joel's prophecies is conjectural.

The Book of Joel is divided into two main parts: 1:1-2:27, dealing with the present: and 2:28-3:21, with the future.

Part One (1:1-2:27) describes a locust plague and drought, calls the people to repentance, and promises the removal of the locusts and the restoration of fertility. An unprecedented calamity has resulted from successive waves of "Northern" locusts (1:2-4). Since food and the means of sacrifice are destroyed, all classes of people are called to mourn (1:5-12), the priests are exhorted to summon the people to the Temple for a national repentance (1:13-14). This calamity is a warning of the approaching day of the Lord (1:15). As food and water are cut off by a drought, the prophet and even the animals cry to God for relief (1:16-20). The alarm must be sounded to warn of the approach of the day of the Lord (2:1-2a). The host of locust is like fire in its devastation

(2:2b-3). They attack the city of Jerusalem like an army (2:4-9). This plague is a foretaste of the day of the Lord and like it, is a divine judgment (2:10-11). The people are called upon to return not only formally but spiritually, to a gracious God (2:12-14). All classes of people are to be summoned and led by the priests in prayer for the removal of the national calamity (2:15-17). The Lord promises the removal of the locusts, plentiful rains and abundant food for man and beast as proofs of his presence and favor (2:17-27).

Part Two (2:28-3:21) predicts the outpouring of the spirit, the signs of the day of the Lord, the deliverance of the faithful in Jerusalem, the judgment of the nations, and the blessings of Judah. God's spirit will be poured out on all ages and classes of his people (2:28-29). Wars and astronomical disturbances will warn of the coming of the final day of the Lord (2:30-31). The faithful in Jerusalem will be delivered (2:32). The exiles from Judah will be restored (3:1), but the pagan nations will be gathered and judged for their cruelties to God's people (3:2-3). The plundering and enslaving by Tyre, Sidon, and Philistia will be requited to them (3:4-8). The pagans are assembled for the final battle with the hosts of heaven (3:9-11). The Lord and his angels will execute judgment on the heathen amid the darkening of the heavenly bodies and the shaking of earth and sky (3:12-16). The Israelites, however, will be protected by their Lord, who henceforth will preserve his holy city from violation (3:16-17). Judah will be blessed with abundant fertility (3:18), but Egypt and Edom will be desolated because of their aggressions against Judah (3:19). Judah and Jerusalem will remain forever; the innocent Israelite blood will be vindicated; and the Lord will dwell in Zion (3:20-21).

The interpretation of the Book of Joel offers three major difficulties which are as follows:

(1) Is the calamity mentioned in 1:4-19 descriptive of a calamity from which the land is already suffering, or is it a prophecy of one which was yet to come? The language of the prophet would indicate nothing but an actual occurrence. He appeals directly to those who have witnessed the calamity.

(2) Are the locusts meant literally or allegorically? Are they locusts or does Joel use them as an allegorical description of a foreign invader? Those who support the allegorical interpretation argue that the description of the effects of the invasion exceeds the bounds of possibilities so far as real locusts are concerned, and that terms are applied to the locusts that are applicable to human beings. They suggest that Joel was speaking of a foreign invader under the picture of an invasion by locusts.

(3) The term "Northerner" formerly presented a real difficulty. The impression prevailed that locust invasions of Palestine came from the south or the southeast. On the other hand, Israel's human enemies, i.e., the Chaldeans, the Assyrians, and others came from the north. This would seem to support an allegorical interpretation of the invasion. Later testimony contradicts such a conclusion. Since accurate records have been kept, it has been found that a number of locust invasions came out of the north. Hence, all later evidence supports a literal interpretation. It is believed therefore, that the first part of Joel's prophecy up to 2:18 is descriptive of a real experience through which his people were passing. The remainder is prophetic and apocryphal.

Message

Joel calls Israel's attention to its sins and insists that a day of reckoning, the Day of Jehovah, is impending. It may be averted only by an immediate and a sincere repentance. He appeals to the priests to repent; they in turn are to call the people to repentance.

Style

The writing of Joel is rhythmic. His descriptions are vivid, powerful, and rich in detail. This is particularly true as he lists the plants and classes of people and animals affected by the locusts and drought (ch. i). Another element in the effectiveness of Joel's descriptions is his use of apt similes and metaphors. The locusts are called a "nation" (1:6), a "people" (2:2-5), an "army" (2:11-25). Their teeth are those of a "lion" (1:6). Their destructiveness is like that of "fire," (2:3). They look like "horses" (2:4); they sound like "chariots," or an "army drawn up for battle" (2:5). The rent heart (2:13) is a striking metaphor for inward repentance.

Date

According to the political and religious conditions indicated, the prophet delivered his message about 400 B.C.E.

AMOS

AMOS ("borne" by God), was the first of the great literary prophets, who prophesied in the days of Jeroboam II of Israel around 760 B.C.E. Of this prophet no detailed biography is available. He was one of a band of herdsmen who lived at Tekoa, a village about nine miles south of Jerusalem. The fact that he was a dresser of sycamore trees (7:14) as well as a shepherd, shows that he was no wealthy "sheepmaster" but at most an ordinary peasant proprietor.

Amos was a devout son of the wilderness. He knew the habits of the lion, the birds, the snakes, and of those who hunted them. His writings also reveal that he traveled widely and observed carefully the economic, political and social life of his country. He had the clearness of insight which comes from lonely communion with nature. It was while he was engaged in his ordinary duties that the prophetic summons came to him: "Jehovah took me from following the flock, and Jehovah said unto me, Go prophesy unto my people Israel" (7:15). Recognizing at once the necessity of obedience to this call—Jehovah hath spoken, "who can but prophesy?" (3:8).

Amos made his first public appearance in the city of Bethel. A scene in chapter (7:10-17) describes the prophet's appearance at Bethel on a high festival, and his prophesying of the swift and utter ruin for Israel (7:1-9). The chief priest of Bethel was not minded to let such speech pass. He bids Amos to leave the city. "O Seer, be off, flee to the land of Judah; make thy living there, and there do thy prophesying. But prophesy no more at Bethel, for it is a royal Temple and a residence city." Amos answers: "No prophet am I, and no member of the prophetic order, but a herdsman am I and a ripener of sycamore figs. Jehovah took me from following the flock, and bade me, Go prophesy against my people Israel."

Israel then was enjoying great prosperity but saturated with moral corruption. The value of human life had fallen so low that a slave brought the same price as a pair of shoes. The ruling classes lived in luxury by oppressing and robbing the poor.

As long as the people attended to their rituals and ceremonies, it mattered not to them that the poor should be oppressed. As Jehovah's privileged people they believed they could win His favor by religious ceremonies even in the absence of justice and righteousness.

Amos plunged into a campaign of accusation. He vigorously lashed the merchants who made their measures small when they sold and their weights large when they bought; who impatiently waited for the Sabbath or festival to be over so that they could resume trading (8:4-6).

The ideas of Amos were far different from the religious views of the people of Israel. The God concept then current was a sort of bargain relationship between themselves and their god. Jehovah they regarded as the national God, Who had chosen them as a people, revealed Himself to them and brought them out of the land of Egypt. To serve Him, they needed only to come to the sacred shrines and make sacrifices upon the altars. In return for this, He would cause the land to produce abundantly and lead their armies to victory.

Amos, however, had caught the vision of a universal

God. To him there was no national God of Israel, but rather a God of the entire world.

Just as Jehovah brought up Israel out of Egypt, so also He brought the Philistines from Caphtor, and the Syrians from Kir (9:7). In all the countries of the world His judgments are abroad (1:2). Sinners cannot escape His vengeance (9:1), and known unto Him are the inmost thoughts of men (4:13).

The closest relationship of God to Israel, Amos stressed, does not mean greater favor, but greater responsibility. The universal God of Amos is not to be bribed by sacrifices. Amos reminds the people that they had no need of sacrifices and burnt offerings. He sarcastically tells them that God hates their feasts; their offerings upon the altar, and their hymns of praise.

What He requires is attention to the simple duties of morality. When offered an elaborate ritual as a substitute for justice and mercy, for uprightness and purity, for sincerity and spirituality, He summarily rejects it (5:21). In such circumstances sacrifices and music are distasteful to Him (5:22). His demand is, "Let judgment run down as waters, and righteousness as a mighty stream" (5:24). So long as righteousness is not practiced by the worshipers, Amos preached, it is simply a form of idolatry, and a multiplying of transgression (4:4).

The fundamental difference between Amos and those to whom he prophesied was one as to what constituted the relationship of Jehovah to Israel. As to the unique character of that relationship he is at one with them: "You only have I known of all the families of the earth." But as regards the conclusion to be drawn from this premise, he and they entirely differ. Their inference was that Jehovah would throw over them the shield of His protection; his is that He will punish them for all their iniquities.

Humble though his origin, brief as was his career, the

herdsman of Tekoa was the initiator of that great prophetic movement that was to transform the religion of the Israelites, and to raise it from an ordinary, tribal cult to a universal faith, an ethical monotheism.

Message

The message of Amos may be broadly described as an impassioned plea for righteousness, a moral righteousness in man corresponding to the fixed moral righteousness of God. He preached the necessity for an ethical revival. He severely denounced formality and superstition; and proclaimed the futility of sacrifices in the absence of integrity of heart and life. However, as stern as Amos' preaching was he did not close without a promise of restoration to Israel by means of a purified remnant.

Style

Amos' prophecies are arranged in an orderly and well compacted form; his Hebrew is generally pure; and his style while simple is full of dignity and power. In his writings we breathe the air of the wilderness, and are kept in close touch with Nature. "The wagon loaded with sheaves (2:13); the lion growling over his prey (3:4); the remnants of his prey recovered by the shepherd out of the lion's mouth (3:12); the bear, more formidable to the shepherd than even the lion (5:19); the snares set for the birds (3:5); ploughing (6:12) cattle driving (4:3); corn winnowing (9:9); the basket of summer fruit (8:1) supply him with imagery" (Kirkpatrick, "Doctrine of the Prophets," P. 91).

Date

The book as we have it, was written around the year 748 B.C.E. at least two years later than the time of Amos' ministry.

OBADIAH

THE name Obadiah means "Servant of God." Nothing is known concerning Obadiah. The circumstances which called for the writing of the prophecy were the attacks on Edom by the nomadic tribes of the desert beginning after the fall of Jerusalem in 586 B.C.E., and ending in the occupation of Petra, the capital of Edom, in 322 B.C.E.

The Edomites were the descendants of Esau, the brother of Jacob. The Edomites were a cruel and warlike people who lived by force. The ancient blessing of Isaac, predicting that Esau would live by the sword (Gen. 27:39-40), was true of the character of the descendants of Esau.

Edom was always a very small nation but had constantly loomed large on Israel's horizon. From the time of Israel's entry into Palestine, Edom was an obstacle in her progress and peace.

When the Babylonians under Nebuchadnezzar made their final conquest against the cities of Palestine the Edomites placed themselves at the side of Nebuchadnezzar helping him bring about the downfall of Jerusalem.

The Edomites rejoiced over the downfall of Judah. While the Babylonians were capturing the city from within, Edom stood guard at the passes in the mountains and cut off the Jews who were trying to escape. All who fell into the hands of the Edomites were turned over to the captors of the city.

The Book of Obadiah, the shortest in the Old Testament, contains the jubilant feelings of Israel as it views with hope the possibility of the downfall of its archenemy, Edom.

Obadiah envisions the complete destruction which is to come upon Edom. His vision coincides with the events of the day. The tribes which dwelt on all sides of Edom were leaguing themselves together to join their force against the Edomites.

Message

Edom had its day. Now the day of Jehovah, the day of the Lord's chosen is coming says Obadiah. Mount Zion, Jerusalem, will be delivered into the hands of the Israelites.

Style

Much of the prophecy is in the words of the Lord directly addressed to Edom. For the sake of vividness, the Edomites are commanded not to commit crimes which they actually had performed. The book progresses from the particular to the general; from the judgment of Edom to universal judgment; from the restoration of Israel to the coming of the Kingdom of God.

Date

The book was composed not long after 586 B.C.E., the year of the capture of Jerusalem and the destruction of the Temple by the Babylonians.

JONAH

THE prophet Jonah ("dove"), is summoned to go and prophesy against Nineveh, a great wicked city. He fears (4:2) that the Ninevites may repent, so he proceeds to Joppa and takes his passage for Tarshish. But soon a storm arises of which he proves to be the cause. He is, at his own request, thrown into the sea, which at once becomes calm. Meantime God has "appointed a great fish" which swallows up Jonah, until, at a word from Jehovah, three days later, it vomits him on to the dry ground. Again Jonah receives the divine call. This time he obeys. After delivering his message to Nineveh he waits in vain for the destruction of the city. There upon he beseeches Jehovah to take away his worthless life. As an answer, Jehovah appoints a small quickly growing plant with large leaves to shelter the angry prophet from the sun. But the next day the plant perishes by God's appointment from a wormbite. Because Jonah pitied the plant, Jehovah pointed out to him his inconsistency in being sorry for the plant (gourd) while berating God for sparing a large city.

By his own grief for the death of the plant, "which sprang up in a night and perished in a night" the prophet is taught the lesson of God's compassion: "How should I not have compassion on this great city, Nineveh in which are more than a hundred and twenty thousand human beings which do not know their right hand from their left, not to speak of cattle?" (4:10-11). With this rebuke the book ends.

The narrative is an imaginative story based upon biblical data and intended for edification. The narrator considered that Israel had to be a prophet to the "nations" at large, that Israel had, like Jonah, neglected its duty and for its punishment was "swallowed" in foreign lands. Through suffering, Israel's sympathy and love would then be aroused and its mission would become clear.

Message

The message of the narrator is that Jehovah's compassion is not restricted to the Jews but extends to all His children. Jonah's bitter disappointment when Jehovah failed to destroy Nineveh is displeasing to God. "The essential teaching of the story is that Gentiles should not be 'grudged' God's love, care and forgiveness."

Style

The Hebrew is of a late period. There are several indications of Aramaic influence. The story is simply told and contains a great deal of symbolism.

Date

The story of Jonah was written about 350-320 B.C.E.

MICAH

MICAH, a shortened form of Micaiah ("who is like Jehovah?"), is called the Morashthite (i.e., a native of Moresheth Gath, a little country town in the low hills between the plain of Philistia and the highlands of Judah). Micah was a farmer. He prophesied in the reigns of Jothan, Ahaz and Hezekiah (739-693 B.C.E.). Two aspects of the age moved the Morashthite, the farmer, to stand forth as a prophet. First, he lived through the exciting times of the series of Assyrian invasions of Palestine. To his mind the Assyrians were the agents which Jehovah was using to punish the oppressive upper classes.

The second and more pressing aspect of the times which turned the farmer into a prophet was the social injustice which prevailed.

The upper classes complacently believed that Jehovah would allow no evil to befall his favored people who maintained His Temple on Zion and so they felt secure as they continued to amass wealth by questionable means. To Micah, however, Jehovah was essentially a God of justice who abhorred greed, deceit and cruelty. In his mind the true people of Jehovah were the honest, hard working men of the countryside rather than the avaricious upper classes in the cities.

Micah makes charges against seven different classes of oppressions. He arraigns the greedy land grabbers and the men who have turned women out of their homes and enslaved children; he charges the rulers with being accomplices at this game of oppression; he protests against the religious teachers who are putting the people to sleep with "soothing syrup"; he lays bare the hypocrisy of the pious laymen who give scant measure in trade and weigh with false balances; he scorns the judges who can be bribed and says that the whole body politic is in danger because it is ruled by bosses who lie awake nights to invent evil schemes.

Message

The prophet's message is contained in his reply to the eager question of the penitent people, who wish to know if it will suffice to sacrifice the first born for their sins: "He hath showed thee, O man, what is good; and what doth the Lord require of thee, but to do justly, to love mercy, and to walk humbly with thy God?" (6:8).

Micah's message, sums up God's demand and man's obligation to Him. Micah gave the world the finest definition of religion.

Style

Micah's literary style is graphic and poetical, yet concise and vigorous. His writings abound in bold interrogations (1:5, 2:7).

Date

The genuine oracles of Micah are dated in 701 B.C.E. The anonymous prophecy in (ch. 6-7) was dated (692-639 B.C.E.) by G. H. A. Ewald in 1867 because of the sacrifice of the first born in the Moloch worship (6:7). A later date presumably about 500 B.C.E., is more probable.

The rest of the Book of Micah is a collection of detached oracles all later than the Exile (586 B.C.E.).

NAHUM

THE name Nahum means "full of comfort." Nahum describes himself as an Elkoshite, or an inhabitant of Elkosh, a village, located on the western bank of the Tigris some twenty miles north of ancient Nineveh.

Nahum's prophecy deals with the destruction of Nineveh the capital of the Assyrian Empire which in 722 B.C.E., destroyed the Northern Kingdom of Israel and, until its own downfall oppressed the Southern Kingdom of Judah.

Nineveh was an ancient city, dating back into the third millennium B.C.E. In 885 B.C.E., it became one of the residence cities of the Assyrian Kings. Under Sargon II (722-605 B.C.E.) it became the capital of the empire. Sennacherib (705-681 B.C.E.) made it exclusively the city of royal abode and a seat of culture and learning.

Nineveh was as brutal as the empire of which it was the heart. Among the atrocities boasted of on the monuments of the Assyrian Kings are the cutting off of hands, feet, ears, noses and lips of captives, and flinging these members to dogs and vultures, cutting off eye lids, to leave the eyes exposed to the merciless sun, tearing out tongues, burning out eyes, burning alive. Nineveh was indeed a bloody city.

The Book of Nahum is completely occupied with the impending fall of Nineveh and the Assyrian Empire, which had so long and so brutally tyrannized over all western Asia.

Nahum prophesies that the Empire Assyria will be punished for its crimes. The streets of Nineveh will be full of unburied slain. The proud empire will collapse amidst the jeers of its former victims and the glory that was once Assyria will fall, like newly ripened figs into the hands of the conqueror.

Nineveh itself fell about 606 B.C.E., under an attack of enemies from the north (Medes or Scythians) and was destroyed never to be restored. With it the Assyrians disappear from history.

Message

The great principle asserted by this prophet is that worldly empires maintained by sheer brute force and inhuman disregard of everything save their own aggrandizement are doomed to perish, and that in the end truth and justice will prevail over every form of wrong. His prediction of Nineveh's fall is based upon faith in God's righteous government of the world. To some extent his message expresses the protest of humanity against Assyria as the incarnation of the spirit of the wild beast. "Behold, I am against thee, saith the Lord of hosts, and I will cut off thy prey from the earth, and the voice of thine envoys shall no more be heard" (2:13).

Singularly enough, his message in no way reflects the social and moral atmosphere of Judah in the prophet's time. The sin of the chosen people, and the need for reform so strongly emphasized by previous prophets, find here no expression.

Style

Nahum's prophecy is poetic in form. "His language" says G. A. Smith, "is strong and brilliant; his rhythm rumbles and rolls, leaps and flashes, like the horsemen and chariots he describes" (The Book of the Twelve Prophets vol. II, p. 91).

The vigor of his style and the realism of his prophecy life the book out of the commonplace and set it on the topmost rung of sublime literature.

Date

Nineveh fell about 606 B.C.E. the prophecy of Nahum was probably delivered shortly before the fall of Nineveh.

HABAKKUK

THE name "Habakkuk" probably means "to embrace." Some say it is an Assyrian word meaning "garden plant." Habakkuk was an earnest, straightforward thinker, eager to know the truth and restless until he found it. He also had a social conscience, and as he looked out upon society, conditions seemed so wrong and twisted, and justice so far from being meted out, that he questioned the old belief that God punishes the wicked and rewards the righteous.

The prophet begins by complaining that his denunciation of the violence, injustice and animosities in Judah are unheeded by Jehovah, who looks on in silence (1:1-4). Jehovah replies that these wrongs shall not go unredressed, and that He is raising up the Chaldeans as the instrument of Judgment.

To Habakkuk this only renders the problem bigger and more acute than ever. Fixing his mind on the character of the Chaldeans—their tyranny, godlessness and cruelty,—the prophet expresses astonishment that the righteous Ruler of the world should not only tolerate such monsters, but even use them as His instruments (1:12-17).

In his perplexity the prophet betakes himself to a watchtower and waits in silence for the divine answer to his plea. It comes in the form of a moral distinction: "his (the Chaldean's) soul is puffed up in pride; but the righteous by his faithfulness (by his sterling character) shall live" (2:1-4). The pride of the Chaldean means his ultimate ruin (2:5).

A final chapter has been added to the Book of Habakkuk, a poem of high order. It most fittingly completes the thought of the prophet, proclaiming in triumphant tones the faith of a man who knows God well enough to rejoice in Him although all outward signs of prosperity should be cut off.

Message

The message of Habakkuk is summed up in the words of faith and patience. His was the strong faith that is reached through doubt, and his was the patience that can endure because it is based upon a faith that will not shrink.

> "For the vision is yet for the appointed time,
> And it declareth of the end, and doth not lie;
> Though it tarry, wait for it;
> Because it will surely come, it will not delay" (2:3)

Style

The style of Habakkuk is highly original and dramatic. The language is refined. His expressions are well chosen. His description of the oppressor in ch. 1:14 is one of the finest things in Hebrew literature. "He has made men as the fishes of the sea, as creeping things that have no ruler. He fishes up all of them with the angle, he catches them in his net, and gathers them in his drag-net; therefore does he rejoice and is glad. Therefore he sacrifices unto his net, and burns incense unto his drag-net, because by them is his portion fat, and his meat plenteous. Shall he forever draw his sword, and continually slay the nations unsparingly."

Date

The majority of scholars adopt the date for this book about 600 B.C.E.

ZEPHANIAH

ZEPHANIAH means ("whom Jehovah hides"). Of the personal life of Zephaniah nothing is known beyond what is given in the title to his book. Two facts are conveyed there; his descent from Hezekiah and his prophetic activity during the reign of Josiah. He seems to have been of royal lineage, his great grandfather-Hezekiah being presumably the King of that name.

That Zephaniah prophesied in Jerusalem can be inferred from the prophecy itself (1:10).

As a fearless man of God, he denounces sin wherever he finds it. He spares neither prince nor pauper in his castigations.

Zephaniah was a nationalist and he lashed in indignation those who were bent on assimilation, sacrificing their heritage for things that profit not. He condemns luxury, the pursuit of money, and declares that salvation will not spring from the great, but from the poor and humble.

Message

Zephaniah was the preacher of Judgment and Salvation. He preached judgment as a means by which divine righteousness could be established on earth. Salvation, therefore, was the end of which Judgment was the means. According to

Zephaniah the moral condition of the age implied, the speedy intervention of the Judge. "The great day of the Lord is near, it is near and hasteth greatly, even the voice of the day of the Lord; the mighty man crieth there bitterly. That day is a day of wrath, a day of trouble and distress, a day of wasteness and desolation, a day of darkness and gloominess, a day of clouds and thick darkness, a day of the trumpet and alarm against the fenced cities and against high towers. And I will bring distress upon men, that they shall walk like blind men, because they have sinned against the Lord: and their blood shall be poured out as dust, and their flesh as dung. Neither their silver nor their gold shall be able to deliver them in the day of the Lord's wrath; but the whole land shall be devoured by the fire of His jealousy: for He shall make even a speedy riddance of all of them that dwell on the land" (1:14-18). In such terms Zephaniah sets forth the terrors of Jehovah's "Day."

Style

The writing is occasionally ornate and marked by a kind of wild enthusiasm. Some of the words and phrases employed are rare. The style alternates between stern denunciation and soothing comfort.

Date

Certain allusions to the state of religion and morals in Judah (1:5, 3:4) make it clear that he wrote before the time of King Josiah's reforms in 621 B.C.E.

HAGGAI

IN 586 B.C.E. Nebuchadnezzar II had captured Jerusalem and burned the city, its Temple, and royal palace. He deported the king, priests, and leading people to Babylonia, leaving only the poorest to remain in the land. The exiles, constituting the more vigorous and intelligent portion of the Jewish people, adjusted themselves to Babylonian life and maintained their national identity and religion. In the midst of their misfortunes both the royal line and the priestly class were preserved in the hope that the time would come when new circumstances would permit them to rebuild a national life in the homeland. This hope received encouragement in 539 B.C.E. when their Babylonian rulers were overthrown by Cyrus. At that time a company of them with the authority of the great king returned to the land of their fathers. They were equipped by the free-will offerings of their fellow-Jews who chose to remain in Babylonia, and were led by their prince, Sheshbazzar.

The returning exiles found a poor welcome and almost insuperable difficulties for many years in their ancestral home. Their earliest plans centered in the restoration of the ruined Jerusalem and the reconstruction of their Temple. They had brought with them the Temple furniture which Cyrus had restored to their possession from Nebuchadnezzar's treasury. The initial purpose of the colony, however, gave way to the more immediate necessity of securing food, shelter, and protection. For two decades they lived in danger of famine, attacks from neighboring peoples, and levies made by passing armies. They were probably reinforced from time to time by additional migrations of Babylonian Jews but the general conditions remained unpropitious and discouraging. Two desires survived among them with varying degrees of fervor. They held to the hope that some day their national existence under the rule of a descendant of David would be well secured and they longed to see the Temple restored as the center of their religious aspirations. The bare struggle for existence absorbed the energies of the colonists for almost a generation until in 520 B.C.E., Haggai stirred their flagging zeal at the time when the Persian Empire seemed to be breaking in pieces.

The name "Haggai" means "festal." This name was probably given to the prophet by his parents because he was born on a feast day. The birth of a child on such a day was thought to be a favorable omen which deserved to be preserved in the name of the child.

Of the personal life of Haggai hardly anything is known. It is believed that he was born in Babylonia during the Exile, received his education there, and came to Jerusalem in one of the expeditions which followed the first band of those who returned.

In 520 B.C.E. we find him in Jerusalem preaching with zeal and enthusiasm, and rousing the spirit of the people to action in the sacred cause of rebuilding the Temple.

Message

In simple, forceful language, Haggai spoke to the Jews of their neglect of the Sanctuary. He earnestly called upon the people to devote themselves to the holy task of building the new Temple, for "the glory of this latter house shall be greater than that of the former" (2:9).

Style

The four addresses which are attributed to Haggai are in poetic form. The introductory passages are prose.

Haggai differs from most other prophetical books in the Old Testament in that while the others are mainly collections of prophetical utterances, Haggai is more in the nature of a report on the prophet's utterances and on the effect they produced upon his hearers.

Date

The book is dated about 520 B.C.E.

ZECHARIAH

THE name Zechariah means, "Jehovah remembered." Whatever we know of Zechariah, we infer from the Book, which bears his name. He is described as the son of Berechiah and the grandson of Iddo. He was a younger contemporary of Haggai and began his mission in the second year of Darius, 520 B.C.E.

The prophet lived in an age in which the spiritual life was at a low ebb, in which the prophetic spirit had almost disappeared, or had been brought into disrepute by cheating impostors. There was an urgent need for some tangible evidence of the presence of Jehovah among his people. Over sixteen years had passed since the vanguards had arrived from the land of exile and no earnest effort had as yet been made to rebuild the Temple. The city itself was being restored to its former glory; fine houses had risen amid the ruins of the national capital. However, the laying of the foundation stone and the erection of an altar on Mount Moriah constituted the only progress made in the construction of the Jewish Sanctuary. The prophet knew that believing Jews everywhere needed this visible evidence of Jehovah's presence and favor as their common center of worship and national sanctuary, that without it they would fall into idolatry and syncretism. The time was at hand to urge the people to a realization of their national destiny. In response to the exhortations of Zechariah and his older contemporary, Haggai, the Temple was completed four years later.

Of vital concern to the prophet was also the spiritual restoration of Israel. He insists, as did the older prophets before him, that the Messianic Era will be impossible as long as there is sin and idolatry in the land. The emphasis in his message, therefore, is on moral and spiritual recovery, on justice and social virtues, on right living and right doing, rather than on ritual and ceremony (7-10, 8-17).

Another important issue was the religious and civic leadership of the newly restored nation. Zerubbabel, the governor of Judah, was a direct descendant of the house of David. The prophet's immediate Messianic expectations centered in him. He was regarded as the "branch" (3-8), the restorer of the Davidic dynasty. Zechariah saw in him the fulfillment of the political and religious aspirations of Israel; he believed the new era to be close at hand, and therefore encouraged the people to change their fast days into feasts (8:19). Joshua, the high priest, also held a position of importance, Joshua was to occupy a place "at his right hand"; side by side, he and Zerubbabel were to usher in the new era.

Zerubbabel never achieved the prominence which the seer had hoped for, and the priestly line, which carried on the leadership of the nation, degenerated more and more into mere formalism and externalized religion.

The Book of Zechariah consists of eight visions interpreted by an angel (1-6) and of oracles dealing with the observance of the fasts (7-8).

In his initial address, Zechariah exhorted his listeners to return to their God (1:1-6).

The eight visions of Zechariah seem to be arranged in three pairs (2-3, 4-5, 6-7), inserted between the first and the eighth.

1. The rider on the bay horse, and the "black," "dap-

pled," and white horses. The earth is at peace and there is no sign of the approach of the Messianic Age, but Jehovah declares that the Temple in Jerusalem will be rebuilt and the Jews will prosper (1:7-17).

2. The four horns (representing the heathen powers) and the four smiths who will break them down (1:18-21).
3. The man with a measuring line to indicate that Jerusalem can have no walls on account of the multitude of men and cattle therein, and needs none, for Jehovah will be unto her a wall of fire (2:1-5). The appeal to the Exiles in Babylon to flee before Jehovah judges that city (2:6-9) and the song of praise for the conversion of the heathen (2:10-13) form no integral part of the visions.
4. The high priest Joshua, attired in filthy garments, is accused by Satan but is acquitted and clothed in rich apparel (3:1-7). An oracle to Joshua announces the imminent coming of the Messiah (3:8-10).
5. The golden candlestick with seven lamps, each of which has a pipe, and two olive trees at the sides thereof. The lamps symbolize the eyes of God, the two olive trees are Joshua and Zerubbabel (4:1-14).
6. A scroll inscribed with curses flies over the land and destroys the houses of the thieves and perjurers (5:1-4).
7. A woman, symbolizing wickedness, is carried to Babylonia inside a bushel measure (5:5-11).
8. Four chariots go forth to the four points of the compass to patrol the earth (6:1-8).

The most characteristic feature of the prophecies of Zechariah is the visions. By them the prophet expresses the truths he received from God. They are personal revelations and the prophet is taught to see in these images a Divine message which he conveys to his people. Prophecy was a different function to Zechariah from what it had been in the golden days of the past.

The visions vividly portray the working of Divine Providence in the world. They picture the restoration of the Exiles and the organization of the new community. They announce the overthrow of the heathen empires and depict the new Jerusalem as the city of peace, her only wall being God Himself. They express the need of Divine forgiveness and foretell the removal of sin from God's people. The visions are of the nature of parables. Certain features in the visions are obscure and have defied interpretation. But it is the lesson in each vision that counts, and that is clear and illuminating.

It may be supposed that the interpretation of Zechariah's visions presented little difficulty to his contemporaries, who would have interpreted them against the background of current events and expectations of the time with which they had a close familiarity. We today who would attempt to interpret them, must inevitably find the details of contemporary life and thought obscured by the distance in time which separates us from the prophet's own time. The most that we can expect to achieve in the matter of interpretation is therefore a fairly clear idea of their general import. The visions have received a great deal of attention from scholars, and widely differing interpretations have been advanced.

Message

He urged upon the people the practice of justice and mercy, and preached that fasting and religious observance cannot take the place of righteousness of character and action. He reminds the people that the return of God to the Temple must be preceded by the return of the people to

God, "Return unto Me saith the Lord of hosts, and I will return unto you" (1:3).

Zechariah is rich in Messianism. "The dominant note of *Zechariah's* prophecies is that of hope and joyful expectation" (How). He promises prosperity; Jerusalem will again be inhabited by thronging crowds, dwelling without defense walls under Divine protection. The Temple will be happily completed; sin will be banished from the land, and peace enjoyed so that the streets will be filled with placid old men and women and with playful boys and girls. He looks forward to the day when the complete Kingdom of God will be established, and the people ruled by *"the Shoot"* assisted by the priest who stands beside his throne. This Messiah, an incomparably greater personality than he could see in Zerubbabel and Joshua, will make a triumphant entry into Jerusalem, and in his day the "new Jerusalem" will arise as the capital of the Kingdom of God on earth, to which the nations of the world will flow and join themselves to the God of Israel and to His people.

Style

"Zechariah was neither a great writer nor a great thinker. Nevertheless, his book is significant as a transition between prophecy and apocalypse and as reaffirmation of the noble teaching of the earlier prophets at a time when prophecy was about to expire" (Pfeiffer). The writings of this prophet are contained in the first portion of the book chapters 1-8. There is no doubt about their unity. On the other hand chapters 9-14 are different in style and diction.

Date

The date of the prophecies of Zechariah according to 1:1 is the second year of Darius' accession to the throne, i.e., 520 B.C.E.

The exact date of the origin of this last section of the book is difficult to fix, but the reference to the Greeks as an important world power (9:13), calls for a date after the battle of Issus 333 B.C.E. Internal evidence points to the conclusion that these chapters contain fragments of prophetic writings which issued at different times from unknown authors.

MALACHAI

THE Book of "Malachai" was originally anonymous and bore the title, "An Oracle the Word of the Lord Unto Israel." An editor added the words "by the hand of Malachi" (my messenger).

Malachai was a simple man, and one whose faith was indomitable. Regardless of present conditions, he believed that right will eventually be rewarded by God and wrong punished.

The prophecy of Malachai affords an interesting and valuable description of the post-Exilic community, with its various currents of thought and life.

From the conditions described in the book, we learn that Malachai delivered his prophecies in Jerusalem (458 B.C.E.) before the advent of Ezra and Nehemiah. It was he who prepared the ground for reforms which they effected at a later date.

Malachi prophesied long after the post-Exilic Jews had rebuilt the Temple, and restored the sacrificial rites. The enthusiasm aroused by Haggai and Zechariah for the Temple had now passed away. The Temple service had fallen into disrepute; the priests had grown careless in the discharge of their duties, the people had become negligent in their payment of tithes and dues. Doubt and skepticism were the order of the day. "It is vain," they declared, "to serve God;

and what profit is it that we have kept His charge?" (3:17). Morals were lax; divorce and intermarriage common.

Malachai faced a difficult situation. His task was to strengthen the tottering faith of his people; to correct the abuses that had robbed public worship of dignity and to put an end to divorces and mixed marriages.

Message

He insists that the Temple ritual be restored, religious obligations met, and priestly dues payed. He vehemently denounces the moral wrongs of his time and pronounces a swift doom upon perjurers and those who oppress the widow and the orphan (3:5). He condemns divorce and intermarriage as acts of treachery against God and the nation. He preaches strict observance of the Mosaic law.

He tells the people that the evils they were suffering were not to be placed at the feet of God, but at their own door steps. He attempts to show them their sins and holds out to them the hope that if they would repent and return, God would abundantly bless them. He would turn them from skepticism to joyous faith.

Style

The prophecy is a series of discussions in the form of a dialogue between the people and the prophet. The dialogue is lively, fresh, suggestive, simple, forceful and direct.

Date

The date of the Book of Malachai can be fixed about 460 B.C.E.

The wisdom of the wise nought can take away. . . . Even among enemies it is a glory, and in a strange country a fatherland.

Apocrypha

KETHUBIM (WISDOM LITERATURE)

THE third division of the Old Testament is designated as KETHUBIM-Hagiographa — Holy Writings — Chochmah—Wisdom literature.

The Hebrew Word Chochmah (Wisdom)

The root meaning of the Hebrew word CHOCHMAH, is to fasten or hold fast, and it includes much more than the word wisdom or its synonyms prudence, sagacity, knowledge, learning.

Wisdom in the Hebrew view was to understand God's works and ways, and to turn one's knowledge of them to practical use.

While wisdom included within its range all God's creation, the department of study that offered the largest return of wisdom was human conduct. It was in this area that the sages mostly worked and were concerned with. The sage never, like the modern philosopher, started with a question. It never occurred to him to ask: Who is God? Rather, he started with an axiom—given a God, knowable, just and wise, then wisdom is to know Him, so far as possible through observation of His works and ways and turn that knowledge to practical account in our relations with Him, and with our fellowmen. To these practical philosophers, the proper study of mankind was man—man in his social relations.

Of all Hebrew literature Wisdom is least distinctively Hebraic. So unlimited by ethnic interests are some of the Wisdom Books, so universal in their appeal, that at least one of them has been thought by some not to have been written by a Hebrew at all (the reference is to the authorship of Job).

It seems that Hebrew wisdom was a product neither wholly of Hebrew nor even of Semitic thought nor designed solely for the Hebrew people. It was not limited by nationality, nor theology, nor forms of worship.

Although Old Testament scholars agree that Hebraic Wisdom is suffused with foreign influence, they also agree that despite the foreign influence, the essence and the spirit of Hebrew wisdom remained undiluted. The most striking assertion of this truth appears in the form of a soliloquy put into the mouth of WISDOM. It appears in the book of Ecclesiasticus 24:3-10 and is as follows:

"I came forth from the mouth of the Most High,
And covered the earth as a mist.
I dwelt in high places,
And my throne is in the pillar of the cloud.
Alone I compassed the circuit of heaven,
And walked in the depth of the abyss.
In the waves of the sea, and in all the earth,
And in every people and nation, I got a possession.
With all these I sought rest;
And in whose inheritance shall I lodge?
Then the Creator of all things gave me a commandment;
And he that created me made my tabernacle to rest,
And said, Let thy tabernacle be in Jacob,
And thine inheritance in Israel.
He created me from the beginning before the world;
And to the end I shall not fail"

The Sages' Method of Instruction

Though we know very little about the personality of the sages, we do know that there was nothing academic about them. They were popular teachers of practical morality. They took their stand in the market place, or by the city gates, and offered instruction to the people by means of parables. Or they collected disciples in their homes, and discoursed to them in proverbs. At first they taught orally rather than the written word. When they wrote, they did so sometimes anonymously, more often under a pseudonym—generally that of Solomon and always their utterances, whether oral or written were of things that hit home.

Purpose of the Wise Men

The purpose underlying all the teaching of the wise was the upbuilding of personal character, the promotion of individual righteousness. How frequent are the exhortations to young people to heed what they have learned from father and mother! Upon fathers they urged what they felt was a wise severity in dealing with their sons. "Withhold not correction from the child; for if thou beat him with the rod, he will not die" (Prov. 23:13).

The wise men rightly assumed that a controlling motive in man's mind is and ought to be his desire for personal happiness. Therefore they strove by all sorts of approaches to inculcate in the pupil the conviction that the individual most concerned in his choice between good and evil was himself. "If thou art wise, thou art wise for thyself; and if thou scoffest, thou alone shalt bear it" (Prov. 9:12). They pictured wisdom as laden with rewards for her devotee. "Length of days is in her right hand, and in her left hand are riches and honour. Her ways are of pleasantness and all her paths are peace. She is a tree of life to them that lay hold upon her, and happy is every one that retaineth her" (Prov. 3:16-18). Interest in others was also used as a motive by the wise men. They appealed to what we may call natural good feeling, quite apart from self-interest. They hold out as lovely and desirable such actions as to gladden one's father and mother (Prov. 23:25), one's husband (Prov. 12:4) and indeed any one else, to brighten the heavy-hearted (Prov. 15:23; 12:25), to avoid causing sorrow (Prov. 12:18), to give life to others (Prov. 10:11), to feed many with satisfying words (Prov. 10:21), to prove faithful to the trust of others (Prov. 11:13), to promote peace and pour forth forgiveness (Prov. 10:12), to guide one's neighbor (Prov. 12:26), to exalt one's city (Prov. 11:11) and one's nation (Prov. 14:34) by one's character.

Aside from emphasizing the personal material benefits that accrue from wisdom, and the satisfaction that affords its user for the enhancement of the welfare of his neighbor, the wise men also aimed to inculcate in their pupils the love of wisdom for wisdom's sake. Who can read the impassioned praise of wisdom in the first section of the Book of Proverbs and not feel that altogether apart from any of her external rewards these men loved her with an ardent devotion? She was at once an ideal to inflame the affection and a possession to feed the mind with inner joy. "Then shalt thou understand righteousness and justice, yea, every good path. For wisdom shall enter into thy heart and knowledge shall be pleasant unto thy soul" (Prov. 2:9-10). "Happy is the man that findeth wisdom, . . . for the gaining of it is better than the gaining of silver, and the profit thereof than fine gold. She is more precious than rubies, and none of the things that thou canst desire are to be compared unto her" (Prov. 3:13-15).

The aim and function of the sage is clearly set forth in the apocryphal book of Ecclesiasticus (39:1-11). Here we are told: "He will seek out the wisdom of all the ancients, and will be occupied in prophecies. He will keep the discourse of the men of renown, and will enter in amidst the subtleties of parables. He will seek out the hidden meaning of proverbs, and be conversant with the dark sayings of parables. He will serve among great men, and appear before him that ruleth: he will travel through the land of strange nations, for he hath tried good things and evil among men. He will apply his heart to resort early to the Lord that made him, and will make supplication before the Most High, he will open his mouth in prayer, and make supplication for his sins. If the great Lord will, he shall be filled with the spirit of understanding: he shall pour forth the words of his wisdom, and in prayer give thanks unto the Lord. He shall direct his counsel and knowledge, and in his secrets shall he meditate. He shall show forth the instruction that he hath been taught, and shall glory in the law of the covenant of the Lord. Many shall commend his understanding; and so long as the world endureth, it shall not be blotted out: his memorial shall not depart, and his name shall live from generation to generation. Nations shall declare his wisdom, and the congregation shall tell out his praise. If he continue, he shall leave a greater name than a thousand: and if he die, he addeth thereto." To the sages, wisdom meant the well trained mind, the disciplined will, the skilled hand, working together for the end of living a sane and normal life.

The Difference Between the Prophets and the Wise Men

The wise man speaks respectfully of prophecy. "Where there is no vision," he says "the people cast off restraint" (Prov. 29:18). Persistently the sages reaffirmed at least one of the characteristic ideas of prophecy—that ceremonial is a poor substitute for righteousness of life, asserting that "The sacrifice of the wicked is an abomination to the Lord:

but the prayer of the upright is his delight" (Prov. 15:8; 21:3,27: 16:6). With the idealism of the prophets, however, they had little sympathy. They say nothing of a future golden age, and seem never to have shared with the prophets the hope of a Kingdom of God on earth. Their general attitude of suspicion toward both the religious idealism and the political radicalism of the prophets is clearly suggested by the advice they give to the young man seeking wisdom: "My son, fear thou the Lord and the king: and meddle not with them that are given to change" (Prov. 24:21).

In the teachings of the wise-men one misses the thundering voice of the prophet, his profound passion, his unshakable determination, his uncompromising demands in the name of Jehovah.

When the prophets contended with the people, the Wise Men were neutral. They were calm and reflective, learned and dispassionate. The truths which became the substance of their teachings were the product of quiet observation. They pondered about human nature and human experience. They considered the fundamental principles of the legalistic and prophetic leaders as the revealed religion, and they came to general conclusions about reward and retribution. Once they came to answers satisfactory to themselves, they consistently voiced them. They expounded the wisdom of adhering to general moral and spiritual laws on the basis of the consequences of disobedience.

The Wisdom literature of the Old Testament will remain classic in the literature of mankind, because it expresses universal truth with aptness and beauty.

THE PSALMS

IN its present form, The Psalms consist of five books, corresponding, according to the ancient rabbis, to the Five Books of Moses. At the end of each book there is a doxology, showing the division. The books are as follows (1) Psalms 1-41, (2) Psalms 42-72, (3) Psalms 73-89, (4) Psalms 90-106, (5) Psalms 107-150.

The poems contained in the Psalter are from different ages and authors. The Psalms express a wide range of religious thought and feeling. In it are reflected a people's heart *throbbing* in its pages. "There is a great difference," said Pascal, "between a book which one individual makes and thrusts into a people and a book which itself makes a people." The Psalms came from the people and they shaped and deeply influenced the spiritual life of the people.

The Psalm Book may be said to be a book of varied moods. In it we find hymns of praise and thanksgiving to God, petitions to Him, meditations about Him, reflections about human life, confessions of sin, expressions of hope, the voicing of sorrow, doubt, joy, confidence and deep faith. These poems embody an inward piety, which characterize the Hebrew mind and heart, the religious spirit of the Hebrews.

The Psalms depict life as it was experienced by the ancient Hebrews. In particular they faithfully mirror the hardships of existence, the struggles of the saintly to remain faithful to their ideals in the face of oppression, the stern fight of the sinner for the victory of his better self, the conquest of despair by undying faith in the righteousness of God. The Psalms echo the thought and feeling, the aspiration and yearning, of numerous men and women of every age, of every generation.

"The Psalms," says Prof. Cornil, "are the prayer-book and the hymnal of Israel; as Israel is above all the people of religion, so the Psalms are the prayer-book and hymnal of the whole world, or at least deserve to be. Of the many treasures that Israel has given to the world, they are perhaps the most precious. They re-echo, and will continue to re-echo, as long as there are men, made in the image of God, in whose heart the holy fire of religion shines and glows; for they are religion become Word. Of them may be said what one of the noblest among them says of the revelation of God in Nature: 'There is no speech nor language, where their voice is not heard: their line is gone out through all the earth, and their words to the end of the world.' "

Purpose

While each Psalm of the 150 in the Psalter may have a definite purpose of its own, yet the Psalter as a whole does not thereby lack in aim which is chiefly to inspire religiosity and provide relief for pent up emotions. For through the aid of this book, both the individual as well as the group are given a chance to talk to and question God. Such an opportunity is not afforded by the other books of the Old Testament.

Style

The Psalms are poetry of moods therefore we find in the Psalms lyrics of all kinds; the pure lyric, the elegy, and the dramatic lyric. However, the one characteristic that is found in all the Psalms, and one that is essential to all poetic expression, is rhythm.

"Rhythm prolongs the moment of contemplation," says William Yeats. The people of the East, were men of contemplation, of spiritual leisure, with a love for lingering on sights and sounds, on images and ideas. Perhaps this is what made for the characteristic trait of Bible poetry, which is commonly designated as Parallelism.

Parallelism means the habit of reiterating or amplifying a thought expressed in one line, by another line following it. That is the chief characteristic of Bible poetry, and it constitutes the style of the Psalms.

Author

According to tradition, David composed all the Psalms. Modern scholars are of the opinion that David wrote only 73 Psalms of the 150 in the book, and that others in some instances identifying themselves as the authors and in other instances ascribing their work to David, contributed the rest of the Psalms.

Date

The Psalter, in the form in which we have it, is one of the latest books in the Old Testament, for it contains poems in which the religious persecution of Antiochus IV and the Maccabean struggle are clearly reflected and very likely events still further down in the 2nd century B.C.E.

The various collections which we have in the Psalter were compiled between the 6th and the 2nd centuries B.C.E.

On the whole, the Psalter expresses the thought, faith, and worship of post-Exilic Judaism.

PROVERBS

THE Book of Proverbs is a collection of sayings of wise men from various ages and times. Aside from the general introduction (ch. 1:1-6) there are eight separate strata in the book, and a number of these have titles which indicate that they were separate collections of sayings of the wise before they were incorporated in the Book of Proverbs. These parts are as follows: a discourse of wisdom, 1:7-9:18; a collection of proverbs entitled "The Proverbs of Solomon," 10:1-22:16; another collection entitled "The Words of the Wise," 22:17-24:22; another, called "Other Sayings of the Wise," 24:23-34; "Proverbs of Solomon, which the Men of Hezekiah, King of Judah, copied out," 25-29; "The Words of Agur," 30; "The Words of Lemuel," 31:1-9; "A Worthy Woman," 31:10-31.

These collections all teach a sound morality. The authors exhibit deep insight into the motives of human conduct. Their instruction is not given in the form of a philosophical ethic but is presented rather in simple maxims, or aphorisms, sometimes grouped upon a central theme, often without any thread of connection. The maxims are based on observation and experience. The pictures of society the authors draw are chiefly of city life with its many attractions, temptations, and vices.

Purpose

The purpose of the proverbs was to serve as a means of guiding and instructing young men. The wise men were fully aware of the many snares which await inexperienced youth and whose attention is claimed by many appealing voices promising happiness. The book then is an attempt to warn youth to beware of the dangers that lie in wait for them and to urge them to make wisdom and common sense their guide in life.

Style

The style of Proverbs is easy and flowing and sometimes even rises to poetic inspiration. The reader is nowhere appealed to on the ground that he belongs to a favored group or has any part to play in the world because of it. He is just a man. The wise men are interested in him for his own sake, because he personally—as every one else—is worth while.

Author

The Book of Proverbs bears the title, "The Proverbs of Solomon son of David, King of Israel." Other titles scattered through the book, prove that it is made up of several collections of proverbs.

That the bulk of this wisdom, should have been labeled Solomonic, is explained by Solomon's fame for wisdom, coupled with the statement that he "spoke three thousand proverbs."

There are several distinct divisions in the book of Proverbs and of only two of these can we be fairly certain about the authorship.

Date

It is the opinion of modern Bible scholars, that the Book of Proverbs was compiled between 350-150 B.C.E.

JOB

IN the opinion of George Foot Moore, "The Book of Job is the greatest work of Hebrew literature that has come down to us, and one of the great poetical works of the world's literature." Tennyson called the Book of Job "the greatest poem of ancient or modern times."

The Book of Job is the story of a man's attempt to understand God's justice—in a universe in which justice is too often meted out to the wrongdoer and the deeds of the righteous more often than not are overlooked by the Ruler of the world.

Job is the story of a man of exemplary piety, but in heaven Satan makes the charge that he is pious because he is prosperous. To disprove this, God permits the destruction of Job's property, his children and his health. Job's patient endurance under these afflictions at length gives way to bitter lamentation. His friends—Eliphaz, Bildad and Zophar—maintain that he is suffering for his sins, but this he indignantly denies. One after another they reason with him, and to each he replies in turn. A second and a third time they speak, advancing from gentle suggestions to specific accusations, while Job, vehemently asserting his innocence, is driven not only into anguished perplexity regarding God's ways but even to outright denial of His justice. Nevertheless, from the cruel dogmatism of his friends he turns again and again to God, increasingly confident that the very One who seems so unjust will ultimately vindicate him. A young man named Elihu enters the debate and eloquently but vainly enlarges upon what Job's friends have been saying. Finally, in the majestic voice of a whirlwind the Almighty Himself replies to Job, reviewing the marvels of Creation until Job confesses that his denial of God's justice was due to ignorance. God then condemns the friends, declares that Job has spoken rightly of Him and restores the sufferer to wealth and happiness.

The chief point at issue in the discussion between Job and his friends is the justice of God in his dealings with human beings.

Job's friends argue that human suffering is a punishment for sin. Job refutes this theory, he sees no relation between man's conduct and man's fate. God's activity, according to Job, indicates that He is not bound by the standards of human justice and mercy.

Purpose

Scholars are of the opinion that the Book of Job was written as a criticism of the teaching of the wise men of Proverbs and their like. The wise men had urged upon their disciples a high standard of ethics. As an incentive to righteous living, they held out the promise of material reward. The hope of material blessings was not the only motive to which they appealed but it was the chief one. They repeated it time and again, affirming retribution to be one of the surest facts of God's government. "Behold the righteous shall be recompensed on the earth; how much more the wicked and the sinner" (Prov. 11:31).

Due to the teachings of the prophets that God ruled His universe with absolute justice, and the further stress of the sages on the connection between prosperity and piety, the belief had become entrenched that God rewards with material blessings those who live virtuously and punishes the sinner with suffering.

The author's purpose is to refute the dogma that all suffering is retributive. He denies that human conduct is justly rewarded or punished on this earth by a just and merciful God. He further aims to teach that the gap between God and man is impassable. "He is not a man, as I am, that I should answer him, and we should come together in judgment." What can a deity, whose power is beyond comprehension, whose wisdom is forever hidden from man, whose works are "past finding out," who is eternal, spiritual, invisible, have in common with a creature as ephemeral, insignificant and miserable as man? Even man's noblest ideals of justice and right are meaningless for God (Job 9:14-20).

Style

Job's command of language and power of expression are unmatched in the annals of literature. He used the greatest vocabulary of any Hebrew writer. The style of the book is highly personal. The author placed in the mouth of Job his own feelings, doubts and hopes. These varying moods are reflected in his style which is rich in contrasts.

Author—Unknown

Date

It is believed that this book was composed between the fifth and fourth centuries B.C.E.

SONG OF SONGS

SONG OF SONGS, (prescribed reading for the festival of Passover), is one of the greatest love poems in the treasury of world literature. The poem describes the deep, true, love experienced by a shepherdess who has fallen in love with a shepherd of the same village. One day the servants of the king (according to tradition believed to be Solomon) chanced to pass through the village of the shepherdess, noticing her, they are touched by her beauty; they lead her away as captive to the king's palace. Fascinated by her charm, the king attempts to win her love. Failing to achieve his end, and sensing her profound love for the shepherd, he allows her to return home. Upon her return, she rejoins her lover—recounts to him her experiences at the king's palace, and assures her brothers that their solicitude for her virtue was unwarranted.

Purpose

It seems that it was the intent of the author to hold up before the children of men, two types of love; the sensual degraded polygamous love of the king, and the pure, holy, genuine, love of the shepherdess. It was this latter type of love that inspired Rabbi Akiba to say that "If the other books of the Bible are holy, the Song of Songs is holy of holies."

In addition to its teaching a lesson on pure love, Song of Songs also serves an allegorical purpose. There has been a great diversity of opinion as regards the interpretation of Song of Songs. Jews see in it figuratively the love between Jehovah and Israel. Christians see in it the love of Christ for his Church.

Style

The verse moves lightly and gracefully, the imagery is picturesque and inspiring. The poet leaves no doubt that he was susceptible to the loveliness of nature. He carries us with him into the open air, to the vineyards, the village and the mountains, and with him we experience sunrise, inhale the fresh morning air, the scent of field, flowers, and pomegranates. As a love poem, it ranks as the greatest the Bible has to offer.

Author

According to tradition, Solomon wrote Song of Songs. Evidence of style and language, however, point to an age later than the period of Solomon.

Date

The language of the book indicates that it was written about 250 B.C.E., or shortly before.

RUTH

THE Book of Ruth which is prescribed reading for the festival of Shavuoth (Pentecost), is a story about a wealthy man who lived in Bethlehem of Judah, and who, because of famine was forced to go with his wife Naomi and two sons, Mahlon and Chilion, to settle in Moab. Within a short space of time, Elimelech dies and also his two sons who married Moabite women. Naomi then decided to return to Judea, and urged her daughters-in-law Orpah and Ruth to return to their respective families. Orpah, left Naomi, but Ruth could not be persuaded to leave her widowed mother-in-law. Ruth's response was: "Entreat me not to leave thee, and to return from following after thee; for whither thou goest, I will go; and where thou lodgest, I will lodge; thy people shall be my people, and thy God my God; where thou diest, will I die, and there will I be buried; the LORD do so to me, and more also, if aught but death part thee and me" (1:16-18). The two women arrived in Bethlehem at the time of the barley harvest. Ruth went out into the fields to glean after the reapers, and by chance found herself on the land of Boaz, a wealthy kinsman of her father-in-law Elimelech. Impressed with Ruth's gentleness and kindness, he takes her for his wife. Ruth bore him a son Obed, who became the grandfather of King David.

Purpose

It is believed that the author, through the story of Ruth, registers a complaint against the narrowness of those who condemned all marriages with foreigners. Thus he shows that King David himself had Moabite blood in his veins.

Style

The Book of Ruth is one of the most charming short stories in Hebrew literature, written in simple and direct prose, it has been likened by students of comparative religion to "a beautiful valley full of flowers, fertile fields and gentle brooks." The Book of Ruth is a superb poem of inimitable grace and tenderness. It is a source book for drama, story, pageantry, art, worship and life.

Author

The author of this book is unknown.

Date

The story of Ruth was written about the year 400 B.C.E., although its unknown author sets it some seven hundred years earlier, "in the days when the judges ruled."

LAMENTATIONS

LAMENTATIONS, referred to by the Talmud as "Kinot," "elegies" is read in the Synagogue on Tisha B' Ab—the ninth day of the Hebrew month Ab, to commemorate the destruction of the first and second Temples.

The Book of Lamentations consists of five chapters—actually five poems. The poems express the sorrows of the people of Judah and Jerusalem at the time of Nebuchadnezzar's capture of the city in 586 B.C.E.

Purpose

Lamentations asks: What is the meaning of the terrible calamities that have overtaken us between 608 and 586 B.C.E.? Can these events really be understood as expressive of God's will? The poems throb with anguish and consternation.

The chief purpose of Lamentations is to teach the disciplinary value of suffering, the absolute justice and abiding love of God, the inscrutability of His ways and the necessity of patience. God's purposes may be unfathomable but dependable.

Style

The five Lamentations differ considerably in character

yet they are linked together by a unity of subject and feeling. The first four poems are in the Hebrew elegiac meter, the verse used for dirges.

According to the elegiac meter, the first member of the verse is longer than the second, from which it has derived the name "limping verse" and so, instead of being balanced and helped by the second, it is echoed by it imperfectly making the whole verse seem to die away in a plaintive, melancholy cadence.

All chapters, except the fifth are written in an acrostic form; that is the poet, describes the sorrows of Israel by starting with the first letter of the Hebrew alphabet and going all the way through to the end. The alphabetic artifice is not uncommon with Hebrew poets.

Author

The poems are not all by the same author; although the traditional opinion is that Jeremiah wrote the book. There is nothing in them that would lead one to think of Jeremiah as the author.

Differences of style and vocabulary both from Jeremiah and within the poems themselves, show not only a different author from that of Jeremiah but also a composite authorship of Lamentations.

Date

It is uncertain whether the author lived during the capture of Jerusalem by Nebuchadnezzar in 586 B.C.E., and recorded the event as he personally experienced it, or whether the time of the writing took place at a later period. Hence a definite, even an approximate date, for the book cannot be set with any certainty.

ECCLESIASTES

THE Book of Ecclesiastes is prescribed reading for the festival of Succoth (Tabernacles) (feast of the harvest).

The Hebrew title of the book is "Koheleth," "one who speaks in an assembly"—the assembly being all who give their hearts to the acquisition of wisdom.

The book opens with the phrase "Vanity of vanities all is vanity!" Life says the author, has nothing of permanent value to offer. His attitude is not one of bitterness but of calm hopelessness, with an occasional tinge of disgust or contempt. He fancies that he has tried or observed everything in human experience, and his deliberate conclusion is that nothing is worth doing. He believes in an all-powerful but indifferent God, and is himself an observer of society, standing aloof from its passions and ambitions, and interested only in pointing out its emptiness.

This general view is set forth in a number of particular observations:

His fundamental proposition is that there is a fixed, unchangeable order in the world, a reign of inflexible law-natural phenomena, such as sunrise and sunset, recur regularly; for everything in human experience a time has been set; all its phenomena are to be regarded not as utterances of a living, self-directing world, but as incidents in the work of a vast machine that rolls on forever; there is an endless repetition—nothing is new, nothing lost; God, the author of all, seeks out the past in order to make it once more present; it is impossible to add to or take from the contents of the world, impossible to change the nature of things; the result is unspeakable weariness—a depressing series of sights and sounds. No goal or purpose is discoverable in this eternal round. To what end was the world created? It is impossible to say. Such is Koheleth's view of the world.

Further, says Koheleth, man is impelled to study the world but under the condition that he shall never comprehend it. God has made the world an object of man's thought, yet so that man can never find out the work that God has done. The reference seems to be not so much to the variety and complexity of phenomena as to the impossibility of construing them rationally or in such a way that man may foresee and provide for his future. Man is in the clutches of fate; there is no observable relation between exertion and result in life; the race is not to the swift nor the battle to the strong (7:23-24); (8:16-17).

Human life, Koheleth declares, is unsatisfying. He inquired, he says, into everything that is done by men under the sun. God has inflicted on men a restless desire for movement and work, yet life is but a catalogue of fruitless struggles. He gives a number of illustrations. In his character of king he tried all the bodily pleasures of life all these he set himself to enjoy in a rational way, but, when all was done, he surveyed it only to see that it was weary and unprofitable (2:1-11).

The whole constitution of society seems to the sage a lamentable thing; the poor are oppressed, the earth is full of their cries, and there is no helper (4:1).

There is no sacredness or dignity in man or in human life; man has no pre-eminence over beasts, seeing that he and they have the same final fate, die and pass into the dust, and no one knows what becomes of the spirit, whether in man's case it goes up to heaven, and in the case of beasts goes down into Sheol—death is practically the end—all; and so poor a thing is life that the dead are to be considered more fortunate than the living, and more to be envied than either class is he who never came into existence. It is a special grievance that the wicked when they die are buried with pomp and ceremony, while men who have acted well are forgotten in the city (4:2-3; 8:10).

His conception of God is in accord with these views. God for him is the creator and ruler of the world, but hardly more; he is the master of a vast machine that grinds out human destinies without sympathy with man and without visible regard for what man deems justice—a being to be acknowledged as lord, not one to be loved. There can thus be no social contact between man and God, no communion of soul, no enthusiasm of service. Moral conduct is to be regulated not by divine law (of this nothing is said) but by human experience.

There are many sayings in the book that appear to be at variance with its fundamental thought. For example, wisdom is praised in a number of passages though it is elsewhere denounced as worthless. It may be said that the author, while denying that wisdom (practical sagacity and level headedness) can give permanent satisfaction, yet admits its practical value in the conduct of life. This may be so; but it would be strange if a writer who could say "in much wisdom is much grief" should deliberately laud wisdom. It may be added that there are in the book a number of aphorisms about fools quite in the style of the Book of Proverbs, some of them contrasting the wise man and the fool; these appear to be the insertions of an editor. Further, it may be concluded with reasonable certainty that the passages that affirm a moral government of the world are additions by pious editors who wished to bring the book into harmony with the orthodox thought of the time.

Purpose

The author's search for the meaning of life, his pessimistic and gloomy observations on life, serve to stimulate thought, and call for a person's examination of his own particular life. If the author does not intentionally or for want of an answer state what man's purpose on earth is meant to be, he challenges men to discover meaning and purpose for their own lives.

The author certainly had a much higher aim than a mere outpouring of his doubt, skepticism and cynicism. It appears from his conclusion that his higher aim was to teach men to lead a better life. Renan said of Ecclesiastes, that it was the only lovable book ever written by a Jew. It is also in many respects, the most profound book in the O. T.

Style

The book may be regarded as an autobiographical prose-poem. There is much warm poetry and music in the book, even though sad and at times depressing. However, because the author's tune is so perfectly true, we do not mind the sadness of the melody conveying the truth.

Author

The traditional belief is that Solomon wrote Ecclesiastes. According to the opinion of Bible scholars, Solomon did not author this book. While it is true that the name of King Solomon does appear in the book, yet, the words of the King in chapter 1:12 relate to one who was King over Israel. "I was King over Israel" (1:12) plainly implies that he was no longer King, whereas we know that Solomon was King as long as he lived. It is believed that the author adopted the name "Solomon" to attract attention because of the association of that name with wisdom.

Date

The book was written between 250-160 B.C.E. Its denial of future life could be regarded as a criticism of Daniel's doctrine of the resurrection presented in 164 B.C.E.

ESTHER

THE Book of Esther, (read in the Synagogue on the festival of Purim), relates of a Persian King named Ahashuerus (believed to be Xerxes), who arranged a celebration for many dignitaries. He invited his queen Vashti—to appear before the banqueting men and she refused to present herself. Upon her refusing to obey, the king is advised to divorce her. In her place, Esther one of Vashti's maidens, becomes queen. Esther is the adopted daughter of a Jew named Mordecai, who had been the means of saving the king from the hands of assassins. But Mordecai falls out with the court favorite, Haman, on account of his refusing to bow down and do reverence to the latter. Haman resolves to avenge himself for this insult; he has lots cast in order to find out which is the most suitable day for presenting a petition to the king; the day being appointed, the petition is presented and granted.

The petition was that a royal decree should be put forth to the effect that all Jews were to be killed, and their belongings treated as spoil. On this becoming known, there is great grief among the Jews. Esther, instructed by Mordecai, undertakes to interpose for her people before the king. She invites both the king and Haman to a banquet, and repeats the invitation for the next day. Haman, believing himself to be in favor with the royal couple, determines to gratify his hatred for Mordecai in a special way, and prepares a gallows on which to hang him. In the night after the first banquet, Ahashuerus, being unable to sleep, commands that the book of records of the chronicles be brought; in these he finds the account of Mordecai's former service, which has never been rewarded. Haman is sent for, and the king asks him what should be done to the man whom the king delights to honor; Haman thinking that it is he himself who is uppermost in the king's mind, describes how such a man should be honored. The king thereupon directs that all that Haman has said is to be done to Mordecai. Haman returns in grief to his house. While taking counsel there with his friends, the king's chamberlains come to escort him to the queen's second banquet. During this, Esther makes her petition to the king on behalf of her people, as well as for her own life, which is threatened, for the royal decree is directed against all Jews and Jewesses within his domains; she also discloses Haman's plot against Mordecai. The king, as the result of this, orders Haman to be hanged on the gallows which he had prepared for Mordecai, the latter receiving the honors which had before belonged to Haman. Esther then has letters sent in all directions in order to avert the threatened destruction of her people; but the attempt is yet made by the enemies of the Jews to carry out Haman's intentions. The Jews defend themselves with success, and a great feast is held on the 14th of Adar, on which the Jews "rested, and made it a day of feasting and gladness." Moreover, a day of feasting is appointed to be observed for all time; it is called Purim, because of the lot which Haman cast for the destruction of the Jews. The book concludes with a further reference to the power of Ahashuerus and the greatness of his favorite, Mordecai.

The Book of Esther, it was long ago observed, is singular among the books of the Bible in that there is no mention of God in it. When Mordecai warns Esther that if she fails her people in its hour of need, deliverance will come "from another place," the word God is ostentatiously avoided; before her great adventure she fasts three days, but there is no suggestion of prayer.

Purpose

The book gives the circumstances under which the festival of Purim originated and the reason for its celebration on the fourteenth day of the Jewish month of Adar.

Style

The language is clear and concise. The description of the characters is vivid and graphic. The story contains a great deal of rapid action, which holds the reader's attention from the beginning to the end.

Author

The identity of the author of the Book of Esther remains unknown.

Date

A study of the language of the book reveals that it belongs to the first half of the second cent. B.C.E. A note at the end of the Greek version says that this translation was brought from Jerusalem to Egypt in the year which corresponds to 114 B.C.E. The earliest mention of the festival of Purim is in II Macc. 15:36, where it is called Mordecai Day.

DANIEL

BEFORE the Old Testament canon was closed one writer appeared who while not strictly a prophet, emphasized most impressively the one persistent characteristic which made it possible for the Hebrews as a people to bequeath to the world their heritage. This characteristic which some philosophers have exalted to the highest place in the ethical category is loyalty. From first to last the watchword of the Hebrews has been loyalty—loyalty to their God, to their family life, to their poor. Many were weaned away by the attractions offered them by other peoples, other gods, other surroundings than their native culture.

The striking characteristic of the Hebrew people is that notwithstanding all apostasy, there did persist throughout the centuries from early nomadic days a nucleus of people so loyal to their ideals that hardship and persecution of the severest kind that history records could not break up and dissipate the truth they had to bring to the world. That truth might have been ground to powder and thrown to the winds, had it not been for their persistent loyalty. And so at the very close of the Old Testament epoch, when once more the Hebrew people find themselves pressed hard on every side and many are advocating the easier road of submission and abdication, a writer throws in his words to help the Jewish leaders as they try to rally the loyalty of their people to their banner.

The name of this writer is Daniel. The name Daniel means ("God is Judge"). The information available, conveys that Daniel was between fourteen and fifteen years old, when he was forced with his three friends into captivity into Babylon. Rabbinic tradition has it that he was of royal descent. He lived to an advanced age and witnessed the return of the Jews from Babylonian captivity to their Holy Land.

The Book of Daniel in the form in which it appears in the Bible is written in both the Hebrew and Aramaic languages. Various explanations have been offered for the presence of the two languages in Daniel. One view is that the book was originally written in Hebrew, and later translated into Aramaic; the Hebrew original was partly lost and the missing portion was supplied from the Aramaic translation. Another view is: the book was written in Aramaic and its beginning and end were translated into Hebrew in order to secure its admission into the canon. The book consists of two parts. The first part (chapters 1-5) deals with stories about Daniel and his three comrades. The second part (ch. 7-12), deals with the visions of Daniel. The stories about Daniel tell how he and his three friends, Hananiah, Mishael and Azariah (whose Babylonians names are: Shadrach, Meshach and Abed-neg'o) were carried captive to Babylon by Nebuchadnezzar (597 B.C.E.), and were made palace servants. One story (Dan. 1) tells how these youths contrived to avoid all danger of eating unclean food, and how God blessed them in body and mind for their strict observance of the dietary laws. Another story (c. 3), describes how the three were saved from Nebuchadnezzar's burning furnace into which they were thrown for refusing to worship an idol. A third story relates (c. 6), how Daniel was cast into a lion's den for praying to his God despite the edict of Darius.

These miraculous deliverances constrain the heathen kings publicly to acknowledge that the God of the Jews is the greatest of gods. The same acknowledgment is drawn from Nebuchadnezzar when Daniel recalls his forgotten dream and interprets it, after all the diviners of Babylon had failed (c. 2); he alone is able to decipher and explain for Belshazzar the handwriting on the wall (c. 5). The stories of Nebuchadnezzar's madness (c. 2) and of Belshazzar's feast (c. 5) teach also how God punishes kings who in their pride of power exalt themselves before Him, or in their arrogance profane His holy things.

All of them thus magnify the God of the Jews as in power and wisdom above all other gods, and two of the most striking of them have for their theme the deliverance from mortal peril of men who stood faithful to their religion against the king's commandment.

The visions in the latter part of the book are all dated, beginning with the reign of Belshazzar, then that of Darius the son Ahashuerus the Mede, and finally that of Cyrus the Persian. The first speaks of four great beasts, explained as four great kingdoms, the last of which attacks the "saints of the Most High," who eventually are aided by God to have supreme dominion (chap. 7). The second is the vision of the two-horned ram (Media and Persia), which is assailed and overcome by the shaggy he-goat (Greece) with a prominent horn (Alexander the Great); this horn is broken off and succeeded by four other horns (the four kingdoms that arose out of Alexander's empire). One of the four horns is to attack the sanctuary and cause the burnt-offering to cease for 2,300 evenings and mornings (1,150 days, or about 3½ years; chap. 8). The third vision is an explanation that the 70 years of captivity predicted by Jeremiah (Jer. 29:10) are in reality 490 years, that is, 70 weeks of years (chap. 9). The final vision introduces the figure of Michael the angel of God, who declares that there will be wars between Persia and Greece, and between the kingdom of the north (Seleucid Syria) and the kingdom of the south (Ptolemaic Egypt). A king of the north will attack the sanctuary, but finally Michael will arise against him and overcome him; the dead will arise from their graves and the reign of righteousness will be ushered in (chaps. 10-12).

The general religious ideas of the book are those of the Apocalyptic literature. Righteousness consists of obedience to the law of God, even at the risk of one's life; but the righteousness of the heroes of Daniel is always that of refusing to bow down to idols or to eat food that is not ritually pure, or of praying three times a day in the direction of Jerusalem; ethical and moral problems are never presented, though truthfulness and integrity are considered high virtues. The righteous are saints of the Most High, and presumably few in number. God is presented as the Ancient of Days; dominion is to be given to a being in human form (7:13-14). Daniel is the only book in the Bible that clearly refers to the resurrection of the dead; this is to take place at the end of the persecution, when all will rise, some to everlasting glory, others to everlasting abhorrence (12:3). The doctrine of the resurrection of the "many" is the most unique contribution of Hebrew literature. There had been a growing belief in life after death, but the author of Daniel goes far beyond the statements of older prophets. For the first time in Hebrew literature we find the doctrine of future reward and punishment and the resurrection of the wicked; it is the necessary outcome of the moral judgment which the author expects of God in vindicating His righteous cause.

No book of the Hebrew Bible has given rise to so much speculation as Daniel. When its prophecies were not fulfilled in the 2nd cent. B.C.E., it was held that they referred to later events.

Purpose

The purpose of Daniel is to point out that God frustrates the plans of the mightiest monarch and defends His servants who in times of danger or temptation remain faithful to Him. Daniel also attempts to impart the thought that the course of history is determined by a divine plan, and that it is part of that plan to end, in God's own time, the trials of the righteous.

Style

Each story of the book has a definite theme which is well developed and carefully carried to a dramatic climax. The writer is familiar with classical Hebrew from which he draws much information and inspiration. "The Book of Daniel" says Robert H. Pfeiffer, "is a great literary monument, the first real apocalypse and the classic example of this literary genre."

The traditional belief is that the book was composed by the person whose name it bears.

Date

Scholars are of the opinion that the book was written between the middle of the fifth century (450 B.C.E.) and the beginning of the fourth and was edited after the Hebrew Canon of the prophets was fixed which took place about 200 B.C.E. Otherwise Daniel would have been included among the prophets. As it is, the Book of Daniel is found in the third division of the Hebrew Bible which is called "Kethubim"—"Holy Writings."

EZRA

THE Jewish community in Babylonia was deeply disturbed concerning the state of religion in Palestine. In the Jewish community of Babylonia, learning flourished, many gave themselves to the study of the Law and the writings of the Prophets. There enthusiasts were not content to have Babylonia the center of Jewish learning and piety. Their eyes were always on their homeland on the city of Jerusalem.

A man who headed the Babylonian enthusiasts and who assumed the role of strengthening Judaism in Palestine was one by the name of Ezra—the son of Seraiah. He is introduced to us by the Chronicler as a priest and "a ready scribe in the law of Moses" (Ezra 7:1).

Ezra was animated by a single purpose. "He had set his heart to seek the law of Jehovah, and to do it, and to teach in Israel statutes and ordinances" (7:10). He was determined to go to Palestine, to Jerusalem and to take charge of affairs there. In order to do this it was necessary to obtain the authorization of the king. Ezra together with a deputation of Jews appeared before King Artazerxes, and upon stating their case, they received permission to execute their mission. As a matter of fact, the king gave Ezra a "letter" which commissioned him to "make an investigation concerning Judah and Jerusalem according to the law of thy God which is in thy land," to appoint judges over the Jews living west of the Euphrates with the duty of enforcing the law under severe penalties and of teaching it to those who did not know it. Ezra was further authorized to take up with him any Babylonian Jews who might volunteer for the expedition and to solicit free-will offerings from the Jewish community for the Temple worship, conveying these, along with the offerings made by the king and his counsellors, to the proper officials in Jerusalem. He was also directed to provide for worthy worship in the Temple, drawing on the king's treasurers to a generous extent if need be. Finally the document ordered that the clergy of the Temple be free of taxation.

His arrival in the capital kindled the zeal of the religious-minded among the people, and his opportunity came for fulfilling the mission he was destined to perform when he learned of the prevalence of the mixed marriages.

His fervent expression of horror excited alarm, and led to the setting up of a commission of elders and the holding of a court of enquiry throughout the country. All foreign marriages were by universal assent repudiated, and a series of reforms were put into effect.

The importance of the reforms lay chiefly in the removal of the Torah from the exclusive possession of the priests and its becoming the common property of the nation as a whole. Its dissemination put an end to what had become the monopoly of a class. The Book of the Law, exerting an intimate influence upon the populace, was now a powerful safe-guard against idolatry, and it set the standard of social life, to the Jew of the Diaspora—(in other lands) as well as to the Jew in Judea. Ezra's reforms marked the triumph of Judaism over the decline into heathenism.

Ezra had a profound influence upon the development of Judaism. Numerous enactments, which were incorporated in the practice of Judaism, are attributed to him by Jewish tradition. "Ezra," says Travers Herford in his book 'The

Pharisees,' "marks in the long history of the Jewish people, the opening of a new period, a new stage of development, as important as the rise of prophecy, and only less important than the work of Moses. If Moses were the real founder of the Jewish religion, giving to it the power to rise above and draw away from the religions of the 'peoples round about,' Ezra stood forth at a most critical period to save the Jewish religion, and with it the national life, from relapsing into decay through contact with Gentile ideas and practices."

Purpose

The writer aimed to give an account of the means used by Ezra in getting the Jewish people to accept God's law as binding, and to show how in consequence of accepting God's law, the community purged itself of all foreign elements and became a community of a particular stamp.

Style

A fair portion of the book is in Aramaic (4:8-6:18 and 7:12-26). In parts the language is pure and vigorous. The story is told in a simple and exciting manner.

Author

It is the belief of biblical scholars that both books, Ezra and Nehemiah, were transmitted to posterity by the anonymous person known as the Chronicler, the author of the books of Chronicles.

Date

The date for Ezra and Nehemiah is believed to be around 350 B.C.E. Support for this date is claimed in the list of high priests in Nehemiah 12:10, which includes Jaddua, whom Josephus claims (cf. Nehemiah 13:28) was high priest at the time of Alexander the Great (332 B.C.E.). On this basis the majority of scholars date the work of the Chronicler 350-250 B.C.E.

NEHEMIAH

OUR knowledge of Nehemiah ("God has comforted") is derived from the memoirs, written by his own hand. With straight forward simplicity and frankness, Nehemiah tells a story about himself—which enables us to follow him with great interest.

We know nothing of the past life of Nehemiah before the beginning of his memoir, when he introduces himself to us as the cup-bearer of King Artaxerxes of Persia (1:1). The personality of Nehemiah, as revealed in his memoirs, is in many respects strangely attractive. He appears as a gifted and accomplished man of action, well versed in the ways of the world, and well equipped to meet difficult situations. The combination of strength and gracefulness, the generosity, fervent patriotism, and religious zeal of the man contributed to form a personality of striking force and power. He is a unique figure in the O. T., and rendered services of incalculable value to the cause of Judaism. He was a man of great wealth and highly regarded by the king whom he served in an intimate capacity.

Though Nehemiah served Persia faithfully, nevertheless his heart was in Jerusalem, "the place of his fathers' sepulchres" (2:3) and in the Palestinian community that had survived the devastating blow of the "captivity" more than a century before. During the period of Nehemiah (445

B.C.E.) things had not been going well in Judah. Lax ways prevailed in the religious life of the community. Mixed marriages were frequent, especially in high circles, and foreign influences were making themselves felt, and the Sabbath was loosely observed. But the crowning wretchedness lay in the condition of Jerusalem. Its walls and gates were in ruins and the area within was covered with heaps of rubbish.

A leader was required strong enough to overcome hostile forces in the environment and rally the people. The miserable condition of the Jewish community in Palestine was brought to the attention of Nehemiah. Nehemiah decided to go to Palestine and do what he could to improve matters in the Holy Land. He obtained permission from the king, and set out with an escort of "captains of the army and horsemen" and in due time presented himself at Jerusalem as its new Persian Governor (2:2). Nehemiah's first task when he arrived as governor with a commission from the Persian king was to rebuild the walls of Jerusalem. He was a man of strong feeling, perseverance and energy. Though his plan was violently opposed by the Samaritans, he succeeded in restoring the walls in the short space of fifty-two days. The entire population had been enlisted for the task and worked day and night.

Nehemiah then turned his attention to necessary reforms. The tribute exacted by the Persian overlord weighed most heavily upon the poor who borrowed from the rich on interest to pay their share. Unable to refund their debts, they forfeited their small holdings and often saw their children sold as slaves to their creditors. Nehemiah abolished usury and compelled the rich to return all mortgaged property to the original owner. He also took steps to populate the desolated capital.

After a governorship of twelve years Nehemiah returned to the Persian court. In his absence his work suffered and the old evils returned. He visited Jerusalem again and instituted resolute measures for their eradication. His was a powerful personality which impressed itself strongly on his generation as well as later generations.

Purpose

The Chronicler's aim seems to point to the fact that Nehemiah, like the prophets before him, sensed God's charge to him and in performing His will felt the "hand of God" guiding and defending him in his holy work (Neh. 2:8, 18). Always Nehemiah was confident that his almost impossible task of reviving the Jewish community could not be accomplished without God's guidance and support.

Style

The narrative is simply told. The language, like that of Ezra, is partly in Aramaic. There is much suspense, surprise and action.

Author

"The words of Nehemiah" are recorded in chapters 1-2, 3:33-6:19; the remainder has been either revised or written by the Chronicler.

Date

The date for Ezra and Nehemiah is believed to be around 350 B.C.E. Support for this date is claimed in the list of high priests in Nehemiah 12:10, which includes Jaddua, whom Josephus claims (cf. Nehemiah 13:28) was high priest at the time of Alexander the Great (332 B.C.E.). On this basis the majority of scholars date the work of the Chronicler 350-250 B.C.E.

CHRONICLES (1 and 2)

THE Hebrew name for Chronicles is "Divre Hayomim" which means "the words of the days." A free translation of the title would be "the events of the times." In the Hebrew Bible, Chronicles is the last Book.

While the author of the Books remains unknown, the contents reveal that he was a priest or a Levite, if not a member of the Temple Choir. We can also infer that the author was a student of history, a statistician and particularly one who was deeply concerned with the religion of his people and their prescribed practices.

The author's gathering of the material, his attention to genealogical data, his detailed description of the Temple worship, his exclusive interest in the Southern Kingdom, his deliberate disregard of the Northern Kingdom, and his idealization of the two great leaders, David and Solomon, all these efforts indicate that the chief purpose of the writer, was to preserve religious formularies and ideals, and to offset whatever may have been the dangers of its being exposed to the pressure of Greek influences.

What significance has the Chronicles for our own time? Does he have something of real value to give? In it he has presented a necessary side of religion, the side that has to do with things of the Temple and with Worship. He stresses the prayer and praise element in worship rather than the offering of sacrifices. He has incorporated into his book much devotional material, giving it warmth and color and religious emotion. One of the loveliest traits he displays is his pervasive note of joy, which of course is a well-spring of praise.

Purpose

The Chronicler's lessons are carefully illustrated by describing the reward of success that came to the righteous rulers, and the disaster and tribulation that befell the godless. For example he shows how David planned the Holy Temple and instituted the Temple worship, leaving behind him a dynasty assured of divine favor forever; how Solomon built the Temple and ordered it according to David's plan; how therefore he prospered; how after his death the self-will of Jeroboam brought on the great schism whereby northern Israel fell away from Jehovah's true religion and ceased to count as a factor in the nation; how the kings of Judah prospered whenever they adhered to the Davidic institutions but suffered through each disloyalty, till at last accumulated transgressions brought about the destruction of City and Temple and the captivity of the people; how under Cyrus a great number of faithful Jews returned from captivity and rebuilt the Temple, but mingling with the profane people of the land, did not prosper; how Nehemiah the governor rebuilt the walls of the City with the help of the people, provided Jerusalem with residents, introduced reforms and restored the full Levitical worship of the Temple; how finally Ezra the priest and scribe brought with him the law of Moses from Babylon and induced the people to undertake its observance, putting an end to the marriages of Jews with aliens and establishing the Temple worship on a sufficient basis.

Style

The style of Chronicles is forced, the language is late Hebrew which has many affinities with Aramaic. It is also characterized by rare new words as well as old expressions with new meanings. Generally it may be said that the standard of the Books falls below that of the other historical books of the Bible.

Author

The author is known only as the *Chronicler*.

Date

Scholars date this writing sometime after the work of Nehemiah and Ezra was concluded, which would be 350 B.C.E. or later if one thinks Ezra succeeded Nehemiah and shortly after 433 B.C.E. if Ezra came first.

THE INFLUENCE OF THE BIBLE

THE BIBLE originated in the Orient; but its influence penetrated every corner of the Occident. The Bible narratives, its characters, its themes and its thoughts, have touched and stirred the soul of layman and statesman, painter and sculptor, literary artist and musical composer from earliest times to our own day.

On Art

When, following upon the conversion of Constantine the Great, Christianity became the official religion of Rome (325), and the great churches were built there, many of the mosaics with which these buildings were adorned dealt with the Old Testament prophets, with Adam and Eve and other Old Testament themes; for, all Scripture was considered one and the importance of the Old Testament as the theological basis of the New was accepted generally.

It was natural that the first paintings illustrating Scripture were made upon the walls of the Catacombs and afterwards upon the walls of the churches, for here was a great expanse ready for the decoration of the artist. The frescoes of Florence are esteemed of primary importance, presenting as they do some of the greatest paintings of the early Renaissance.

On the wall of the Campo Santo, Pisa, is that painting of the *Tower of Babel* by Benozzo Gozzoli, showing how great was the interest in the Old Testament in those early days of the development of the art of painting.

To the Italian Michelangelo, we are indebted for the titanic statue of *David,* one of the marvels of all time. Rembrandt Van Rijn, has given the world an overpowering painting of *Moses Breaking the Tablets of the Law.* Turner is famous for his depiction of the *Deluge,* the *Destruction of Sodom* and the *Death of the First Born.* Palma Vecchio was one of the earliest to utilize the love story of *Jacob and Rachel.* The water color illustrations of the Old Testament by James Tissot are world famous. William Blake was signally successful with his complete set of illustrations of Job. Perhaps the most popular of all Bible illustrators was Gustave Doré of whose woodcuts many editions have appeared in all lands.

On Drama

Biblical drama did not flourish in ancient times. Rome soon dominated the world, and Roman drama was chiefly an imitation of the "New Comedy" of Greece, which made fun of contemporary society, but shunned anything more profound. This type of play later passed away, and for almost a millennium the drama was a neglected art in Europe.

Toward the end of the Middle Ages the Church revived the drama. Simple plays in Latin, which dramatized the stories of such festivals as Christmas, Good Friday and Easter, were acted in the churches. Later each country—England, Spain and Italy, then France and the German states—developed its own national drama, still religious in content, but written in the vernacular and tinted with national characteristics. In England, as the drama moved from the interior of the church to the churchyard and finally out of the jurisdiction of clerical authorities altogether, it became a vehicle for telling the stories both of the Old and New Testaments to large masses of the populace.

On Literature

The popular appeal of Bible incidents and characters are proverbial. The story of Samson has stimulated some of the great men of letters to dramatic effort. Of these the best known is John Milton's *Samson Agonistes.*

Carlyle spoke of the Bible as one book wherein for several thousands of years the spirit of man has found light and nourishment, and interpreting response to whatever is deepest in him. His *Sartor Resartus* is founded on a passage of Scripture: "As a vesture shalt Thou change them, and they shall pass away" (Ps. 102-27).

Wordsworth admired the prophetic and lyrical parts of Scripture. Macaulay regarded the Bible as "a book which if everything else in our language should perish, would alone suffice to show the whole extent of its poetry and power."

Charles Lamb had a curious knowledge of the Bible which he freely quotes in his essays. Nathaniel Hawthorne reflects a close acquaintance with the Bible. Ruskin declared that his knowledge of the Bible by heart made it impossible "even in the foolishest times of youth to write superficial or formal English" (cf. St. Mark's Rest). Walt Whitman said: "My own essential model was the rhythmical patterns of the English Bible."

On Music

The Bible has been a fountain of inspiration to composers. Étienne Henri Méhul, a well known French composer, achieved his greatest work in an opera entitled *Joseph in Egypt.*

Two operas were composed depicting the story of Moses: one is by the famous Italian Geoachino Rossini, and the other, by the Russian Anton Rubinstein.

The most celebrated musical work to stem from the Book of Judges is Felix Mendelssohn's greatest masterpiece *Elijah.*

The Psalms have tempted composers of every age to translate their lyric quality into tones. Mendelssohn produced an entire library of Psalm compositions.

A beautiful musical setting of Psalm 23 (The Lord is my Shepherd), was made by Franz Schubert. Psalm 137 (By the Waters of Babylon), has been given effective musical treatment by Charles Martin Loeffler and Ernest Bloch.

From the Apocrypha composers have also taken inspiration for their works. Oratorios on *Judith* were composed by Charles Parry, Arthur Honegger and Alexander Serov. The story of the Maccabees was treated in an opera by Rubinstein and in an oratorio by Handel, *Judas Maccabeus.*

On Law

Even in law, in which the genius of Rome was ultimately to exercise so supreme an influence, on European legislation, the Bible in the beginnings had its word to say.

Woodrow Wilson, in his treatise on the State, draws marked attention to this aspect: "It would be a mistake to ascribe to Roman legal conceptions an undivided sway over the development of law and institutions during the Middle ages. The Teuton came under the influence, not of Rome only, but also of Christianity; and through the Church there entered into Europe a potent leaven of Judaic thought. The Laws of Moses as well as the laws of Rome contributed suggestion and impulse to the men and institutions which were to prepare the modern world."

Not alone has the Bible had influence upon European

law, it has affected even more strikingly, the law making institutions of the Occident. The constitutionalism of modern Europe and the United States, can be distinctly traced back to the constitutional struggles of England in the Seventeenth Century, and every one knows that at the back of the parliamentary movement was the inspiration of the Bible.

On Language

How deeply the Bible has sunk into the folk soul of the Occident, is shown perhaps most conclusively by its ingrained influence upon the language of the peoples. Quite apart from the fact that the heroes of the Bible—Adam, Noah, Abraham, Jacob, Joseph, Moses, Samson, Saul, David, Solomon, and the rest—have taken the place of the old mythical heroes of the Sagas and national legends, the phraseology of daily life in all the Western languages bears traces of biblical influence. Whenever we speak of "a land flowing with milk and honey," "a still, small voice," "a tale that is told," "darkness which may be felt," "vanity of vanities," "law of the Medes and Persians," "a wife of one's bosom," "an apple of one's eye," we are repeating biblical expressions. Whenever we "eat, drink, and be merry," "take sweet counsel together," "grind the faces of the poor," "cause the widow's heart to sing for joy," "make a covenant with death," "heap coals of fire," and "be weighed in the balances and found wanting," we are unconsciously plagiarizing the Bible. Much of our popular wisdom comes from the same source, as, for example, "Put not thy trust in princes"; "Go to the ant, thou sluggard"; "Answer a fool according to his folly"; "A wise son maketh a glad father"; "Be not righteous over much"; "A soft answer turneth away wrath"; "The race is not to the swift"; "Love is strong as death"; "In the multitude of counsellors there is safety"; "Righteousness exalteth a nation."

On Religion

However, it is not merely on the externalities of the arts, language and institutions that the Bible has left its deepest impress. Western religion taken in its broadest sense is the religion of the Bible. The religion of the Bible freed mankind from that worship of Luck and Fate which is at the basis of all savagery. It recognized that human affairs and human character were ruled by high principles which soared above individual existence and bound men together in common allegiance to noble ends; it further connected each individual soul with the source of these principles—the Ruler of the universe. Human nature was at once dignified by this notion of personal communion with the Highest Being, while at the same time it was deepened and solemnized by a sense of sin as treason toward the Spirit of the Universe.

The influence of the Bible on Western culture reaches its culmination of course in its monotheism. The worship of the Lord of the universe has now become so ingrained in the Occidental mind, that it is difficult to realize the reverence paid to the multitude of local deities which characterized the classical world.

A necessary extension of the idea of the Divine unity is that of the equality of ALL before the One God. This concept ultimately gave rise to the idea of the brotherhood of all peoples. The brotherhood of peoples makes abhorrent the idea of internecine war. All the dreams of universal peace that have stirred mankind down to our own day are to be traced back to that Messianic vision of the Prophet Isaiah, of an age when "nation shall not lift up its sword against nation, nor shall they learn war any more." To us today it may seem trite, but there was an epoch-making originality in this idea in an age when conquest was regarded as the natural right of the stronger, and a victorious war the ideal of every powerful state.

The overwhelming passion for righteousness is insisted upon in the Bible almost as much as the monotheistic idea, for the one is the concrete expression of the other. The God of the Bible—is no impersonal deity, indifferent to men's affairs nor yet a selfish one, swayed by flattery and bribes; but a God who loved goodness, who abhorred oppression, who laid down positive standards of conduct between man and his fellow, Who insisted on justice, truth and morality.

The ideals of social justice, which Western reformers are endeavoring to carry into practice in our own day, are the ideals taught by Isaiah, Amos, and Micah, now part of the common heritage of the Western World.

Conclusion

Chief among the contrasts which differentiate the Bible from the Sacred Books of the East is the notion of progress. Practically all the peoples of the Orient, in their early beginnings regarded what was as the norm; they could not conceive of change either in the past or the future. As against this, the Hebrew prophets, with splendid indignation, regarded the present condition of their nation as abominable, and felt a confident hope that the divine plan of the universe involved an amelioration not alone for themselves but for the whole world.

PART II

INTRODUCTION

THE purpose of this section of *A Pathway to the Bible* is to encourage one to read the Book with a better understanding of its background, authors, and message. It is not to discuss or to promote either an interpretation or a theology of the New Testament.

The Protestant speaks of the Scriptures as the authority for his faith. Each individual has the duty to seek out his belief through the Book itself. One exposes oneself to God's Spirit through the Bible as God's Word and the Church as a servant of that Word.

The Catholic sees the authority of his faith in the Church and holds that the Church as God-ordained carries the responsibility of interpreting the Holy Scriptures. Tradition tends to be given a far higher status than in Protestantism, for there is an official Catholic way to interpret the Bible in the light of the approved tradition.

The Orthodox finds his interpretation of the Scriptures in the tradition and authority of the Church, as does the Catholic, but with a lesser emphasis upon the conclusive nature of the Church as final arbiter of all scriptural matters. This thinking is something of a bridge between the Catholic and the Protestant viewpoint.

The above statements are broadly put and could be subject to critical variations in definition by the various Faiths involved. However, the objective is not to play spokesman for any Faith, but to remind the reader that there are these different viewpoints concerning biblical evaluation, and that the important thing is that we are seeking to know God's will and to be faithful to His self-disclosure.

M. B. S.

THE NEW TESTAMENT

What It Is

THE New Testament consists of twenty-seven books which are the sacred writings of Jesus' immediate followers and their disciples. This volume, plus the Old Testament, makes up the Bible for the Christian community.

The term "bible" originates in the Greek word *biblia* meaning library. Hence, the Bible is the basic Christian library.

The word "testament" means covenant, compact, or agreement. The New Testament is a new agreement between God and Man, originating in and inspired by Jesus. It is concerned with man's waywardness, his rebellion against God, his pride in his self-sufficiency, and his refusal to surrender his will to God. These sins are not sickness, but a willful revolt, and the New Testament points to the way of reconciliation in Christ: "God was in Christ reconciling the world to himself" (11 Corinthians 5:19).

Because of the sacred aura that has developed around the Scriptures, some people worship the book rather than seek out God's Word. Others are indifferent to Holy Writ. Both these stances are abuses, and serve to block real openness to the faith the Bible has to share.

The New Testament should be read with several major purposes in mind:

1. As a volume overflowing with human insight into man's predicament as he relates himself to his world, his neighbor and his Maker.
2. As a biography of man depicting life situations of suffering, joy, disappointment and triumph.
3. As a history of God's quest for man and man's search for God. God is acting in history, revealing himself in Jesus Christ.
4. As a covenant depicting God's purpose, love and concern for man and man's surrender, submission and final freedom within the divine will.
5. As a testimony of Christ revealing to man the nature of God in personality—a Godlike Christ and a Christlike God. "For it is God who said, 'Let light shine out of darkness,' who has shone in our hearts to give the light of knowledge of the glory of God in the face of Christ" (II Corinthians 4:6).

The New Testament becomes more than a sacred object, it becomes a pathway to God. With this in mind, we must visualize it in its contemporary setting. The Aramaic language, rich in idioms and power of expression, was first used in the telling of Jesus' words and works. But very soon this earliest reporting was put into Greek, the language in which our present Gospels and all the rest of the New Testament were written.

Since that period the New Testament has been translated many thousands of times. The whole of it has been printed in hundreds of languages and parts of it in more than a thousand tongues. It is history's Greatest Story—God came among us to restore our broken relationship with him.

THE NEW TESTAMENT CANON

How the Books Were Chosen

HOW did the New Testament finally become a single volume acceptable to Christians everywhere? It is a fascinating story! No one person chose the books, neither were the contents assembled at any one moment of time. The acceptance of the twenty-seven books as worthy parts of the new "Covenant" (which is what "Testament" means) was a process involving inspired men and churches as well as centuries of time. In a very profound way God gave guidance to the editing of His Holy Word.

There are known to be over one hundred other books in early Christian literature. Why were they not included? Because this principle of selection was used in the churches and such books were found to be of inferior worth for worship and instruction. The early Church Fathers sought to establish a library of acceptable teachings and doctrines, and their choice was a ratification of the churches' everyday experience of choosing. We Christians believe that the Holy Spirit was in this choosing just as he was in the writing of the "canonical" books.

Let us for a moment turn back the pages of history. It is the year 96 A.D., and we are gathering with a small body of Christ's followers in a private home. We are awed and a bit frightened by the occasion, for it is against Roman law to assemble in a worship service. But our convictions have forced us to defy Rome's authority and respond to the call of the Spirit.

After singing a few hymns and offering prayers, we reach a moment of great expectation. Curtains are drawn from the cabinet in front of us revealing the sacred writings of the Jews plus the new literature of the Christian community. These include the words of Jesus, the story of his life, and some writings from his followers. We listen intently, little realizing that centuries later other men will be hearing these sacred words read from Bibles in a multitude of languages, printed by machines and circulated in the millions. Thus we witness the wondrous beginnings of the New Testament.

At first only the Gospels and the Old Testament were read in the order of worship. Later the letters of Paul and others were included. Finally these writings became "The Holy Bible," the Christian's sacred literature.

What makes a book eligible for canonization? The early Fathers also asked this question and came up with several pertinent rules:

1. Was the book in common usage in public worship?
2. Was it traditionally acceptable among the various churches?
3. Was it of apostolic authorship?
4. Did the book or letter establish doctrinal authority as against heretical teachings?

Such considerations seem as valid today as they did then, so we begin to understand why all churches, East and West, came to accept, in common, the twenty-seven books of the New Testament.

Early Canons

One of the earliest known canons came to light in the

year 1740 through the findings of the Monk, Muratori, who discovered some biblical fragments in a Common Place book of the seventh or eighth centuries. A reference to Pius I, who died in the year 157, dated the following scriptural material as acceptable to the Early Church and as in use before this time: the four Gospels, Acts of the Apostles, the thirteen Epistles of Paul, the Letters of Jude and John, the Book of Revelation, also the Book of Wisdom, the Apocalypse of Peter, and several other volumes. It is true that some books of the New Testament were not mentioned and others were added, but the fact remains that the process of sifting the early writings was well along.

Three Fathers of the Early Church should be remembered when referring to the canonization of the New Testament. Eusebius, A.D. 264-340, considered the following books as acceptable: The Four Gospels, fourteen Epistles of Paul (Epistle to the Hebrews was mistakenly included as a Pauline writing), the Epistles of James, Jude, First and Second Peter, and First, Second and Third John. About A.D. 365, Athanasius had given approval to all the present books of the New Testament as divinely inspired and proper scripture for the Church. Augustine, A.D. 354-430, specified rules for judging scripture as acceptable, and gave firm support to the New Testament as we know it today.

About four hundred years after the death of Christ, Jerome edited the Bible in Latin for "common" use (so, the "Vulgate" version). His choice of books plus Augustine's support made the present Canon certain.

From the beginning the choice of books has been subject to honest and capable scholarship and tested in the fire of Christian experience. Of all the enchanting and inspiring sorties into history, few can compare to that challenging pathway which leads to the Bible.

A NOTE ABOUT THE GOSPELS

JESUS was inconsequential in Roman annals. Roman law considered him just another criminal condemned to die. He was quickly forgotten as an annoying and troublesome detail in colonial administration. In fact, we have no Roman records concerning the crucifixion and therefore must depend for our information almost entirely upon a small band of disciples, who saw more clearly than their oppressive rulers the significance of Jesus of Nazareth. To the Romans he was a troublesome Jew. To his followers he was the Son of God.

In other words, Jesus was important only to those who were inspired by his message of redemptive love. They had a story to tell, so they propagated the "Good News," at first orally, then later on scrolls and codices which were read in worship along with the Old Testament.

The Gospels of Matthew, Mark, Luke and John are obviously not intended as complete biographies of Jesus. They are plain stories of an extraordinary man in whom God comes alive—God incarnate in human personality. The authors of the Gospels do not presume to have full knowledge of Jesus. Furthermore, both directly and indirectly they indicate the limited scope of their writings. But they all emphasize the infinite grace of God as revealed in Christ. Their narratives are conditioned by the nature of their personalities and the purpose of their writings—a fact which makes for both humanity and vitality.

From earliest times the first three Gospels have been studied together, revealing common background sources as well as profound differences in materials. Comparative studies have led to the following speculations:

1. Matthew and Luke used Mark as their major source of information but also turned to two or possibly three other sources—
2. Or, they may have had, along with Mark, a common source of documents not known today—
3. Or, these sources may have been unwritten ("oral tradition").

The Gospel of John is obviously quite different from the first three. Though complementary rather than contradictory, it does indicate the use of other source material and has a different cast.

It seems certain at present that this mystery of sources will not be easily resolved. What is far more important is to note that the authors were inspired to use creatively the materials available to them.

THE GOSPEL ACCORDING TO MATTHEW

NO other Gospel is as fruitful in the teachings of Jesus. More than half of this book deals with Christ's message. The basic truths of the Christian faith clothe every parable and speak from every page.

Content

In the opening paragraphs Matthew points out emphatically the messianic nature of Jesus, thus establishing a direct relationship between God's chosen people of the Old Testament and God's chosen Son in the New. Jesus becomes the messianic fulfillment of David's lineage. "The book of the genealogy of Jesus Christ, the son of David, the son of Abraham." (Matthew 1:1)

Then follows a biographical picture of Jesus, his preaching, his rise to prominence, the collapse of his popularity culminating in the crucifixion. Matthew in this manner tells the story of Christ's call, commitment and full surrender to God in the experience of the cross.

Let us now take a structural look at the contents:

The first three chapters reiterate several times the prophetic fulfillment of Jesus' birth and life. Jesus is the long-awaited Messiah. The virgin birth, his baptism and the temptation are revelations of divine purpose as prophesied in the Old Testament.

The fourth chapter deals more specifically with Jesus' activities in Galilee following the imprisonment of John the Baptist.

His teachings are expounded in the Sermon on the Mount (Chapters 5-7), wherein he speaks of the spiritual requirements demanded of his followers, clearly stating the nature of the kingdom and the method of gaining entrance. Although Christ considers the kingdom of heaven a spiritual experience, it is well to note that he also looks upon it as a physical reality. He refers to the kingdom thirty-eight times,—hardly an incidental part of his message. However, the inner aspect is basic: the kingdom "on earth" is first and foremost "in your heart."

In the eighth chapter the author is validating Christ's message by depicting his unique power. Jesus cures leprosy, palsy, fever, paralysis, an issue of blood, blindness and demoniacal possession. Even his power over nature and death are demonstrated in the latter part of the eighth and the beginning of the ninth chapters (8:26 and 9:23-25).

He also endows the Twelve (Matthew 10) with power to heal in his name. Thus inferentially, if not directly, Jesus is pictured as the Messiah whose divine power is victorious over sicknesses of body and of soul. This unique authority, from Matthew's standpoint, was not flaunted as irresponsible showmanship, but was given as evidence of the power of faith made known in Christ.

Unfortunately, many unusual sects and hysterical outbursts have resulted from those who have accepted such manifestations of power for their own sake. Careful reading of Matthew shows conclusively that this was not his purpose.

Excepting Chapters thirteen and twenty-eight, the balance of the Gospel concerns the people's rejection of Jesus, Herod's imprisonment of John the Baptist, the uncertainty of the disciples, and the militant opposition of the Herodians, the Pharisees and the Sadducees.

Chapter thirteen is rich in parables wherein Christ conveys his message of the Kingdom as he visualizes it in the future. In everyday idiom and narrative he proclaims truth, both obvious and hidden, that the receptive might understand and the antagonistic be confounded. The eight parables are the Soils, the Wheat and the Tares, the Mustard Seed, the Leaven, the Treasures, the Pearl, the Net, and the Householder.

More and more the cross becomes the focus of Christ's attention and thought. Finally, in chapters twenty-six and twenty-seven, Matthew brings us face to face with the Passion and Death of Jesus.

A very moving and victorious climax is reached in Chapter twenty-eight when Mary Magdalene and the other Mary come face to face with the risen Christ. Then follows the challenge of the Great Commission, when Jesus appears before the confused and amazed disciples: "All authority in heaven and on earth has been given to me. Go therefore and make disciples of all nations, baptizing them in the name of the Father and of the Son and of the Holy Spirit, teaching them to observe all that I have commanded you; and lo, I am with you always, to the close of the age" (Matthew 28:18-20).

Message

The Law of the Old Testament is not abrogated or destroyed but rather is fulfilled in Christ. Jesus transcends the moral legalism of his day and insists upon an inner moral authority, a righteousness that makes the Law symbolic. Life is to be inspired, governed and judged from within by the law of love. Love and holiness, therefore, become the greater law, transcending all outer legal emphasis.

Jesus and his teachings become the spiritual spring, the waters which can quench man's religious thirst. The kingdom is to be found in the knowledge of God revealed in Christ. Jesus breaks through the smug satisfaction of the status quo, insisting that something more than ideals or religious law is necessary to redeem man from sin. Man's hope of the Kingdom rests in Christ, the Messiah. Faith in him is redemptive.

Matthew seems to have four main objectives:

1. To relate Jesus to Old Testament prophecy—
2. To picture him as a spiritual king of the royal lineage of David—
3. To make certain that the converts in Antioch know the spiritual importance of the kingdom of God—
4. To indoctrinate the Church in the faith that Christ is indeed the Son of God.

Author

There is no firm evidence to establish Matthew-Levi as the author except the tradition of the Early Church, which has frequently found support in historic fact. Matthew was a tax collector and one of the twelve disciples. As a Palistinian Jew he spoke Aramaic, and some authorities contend that this Gospel was originally written in that language. We can reasonably assume that Matthew-Levi was the author and that the book was written in Antioch.

Date

If Matthew anticipated the impending destruction of Jerusalem, the book was written before A.D. 70, perhaps as early as the year 50. If so, then Matthew was writing during the reign of Nero, addressing himself to non-Palestinian converts. If, however, the little apocalypse (Chapters 24 and 25) describe what really has already happened, Matthew may have been written as late as 85-95.

THE GOSPEL ACCORDING TO MARK

MARK is not interested in Jesus' birth, parentage, or even his youth. He ignores these biographical details so as to report the action and words of Christ. This disinterest in details is emphasized by his indifference to chronological order. His one concern is to report Peter's teachings about Jesus. He seems anxious that we know what happened rather than when it occurred. Mark is not a biographer but a reporter.

Content

Let us quickly outline the main events. Mark first reports the good news of John the Baptist. Afterward Jesus is baptized by the evangelist and accepts his designation as the Messiah. Directly Jesus undergoes the temptation in the wilderness which is climaxed by his victory over Satan. Thus the author abruptly establishes the mission of Jesus to the world. All of this and more Mark crowds into the first chapter.

In the remaining chapters we are given a few sections of teachings, several incidents in Galilee, a confession of Peter who recognizes Jesus as the Messiah, and the story of the Transfiguration. Then follows the saving death of Jesus, the discovery of the empty tomb and the flight of the frightened women. The book ends with questionable abruptness, indicating that passages are missing from the original scrolls.

The King James Version has added twelve verses, nine through twenty, to Chapter sixteen. It is now quite universally agreed that these were not written by Mark but were added later to smooth out the text. The end of the original scroll had probably worn away and the final passages were lost.

Mark's Gospel is precise, and to the point. A practical, everyday Roman would readily understand and be interested in his manner of writing, much as you and I find a newspaper report fascinating reading today. The author is concerned with action and therefore describes the works of Jesus, with emphasis on the events of the week preceding his death. And so we find Christ's Gospel revealed in the episodes and events of his life. Mark is a good propagandist become reporter.

Message

John Mark, the Evangelist, strongly stresses Christ's true humanity. He writes of Jesus' bodily exhaustion, of his eating and drinking, and in other ways indicates the Lord's earthly nature. But more important than such physical evidence are the mental and emotional reactions. Jesus feels and responds humanly. No other Gospel is more emphatic in picturing Jesus as a man of compassion, love and even anger (Mark 1:41 and 43). Grief and agony are likewise mentioned. Jesus discloses limitations of knowledge regarding the Day of Judgment and of being under human restrictions in other ways. Matthew and Luke, however, make no such references to his earthly frustrations. Some will explain away these facts, contending that they are self-limitations to fulfill the plan of salvation. But as one carefully considers

Mark's Gospel, he sees more and more the importance and relevance of Jesus' humanity.

Again, we see how picturesque and touchingly natural Christ can be when Mark tells of his taking little children into his arms and blessing them (9:36 and 10:16). Even the Transfiguration and the raising of Jairus' daughter are told as though Mark were there, an eye-witness and recipient of the news at the very moment it occurred. There is a tenderness as well as a refreshing bluntness in Mark's writing.

Mark also emphasizes the divinity of Jesus. Though he speaks of his human limitations, he also credits the Master with superhuman authority, particularly in his capacity to forgive sin. He mentions the Lord's ability to foresee men's thoughts (2:8, 8:17, 12:15) and future events (8:31, 14:27). Finally, the Evangelist firmly supports the sinlessness of Jesus, thus establishing beyond doubt Christ's divine nature.

Mark's Gospel is a vigorous testimony of faith, of Jesus as the Son of God, and of the redemptive power of Christ's martyrdom and resurrection. The book is keyed to great expectation: "The time is fulfilled, and the kingdom of God is at hand; repent, and believe in the gospel" (1:15).

Author

This Gospel does not name its author. As in the case of Matthew, we must rely upon traditional sources and the meager references of the New Testament. The Book of Acts is our richest source of information about John Mark, the traditional author of this Gospel.

He came from a Christian family in Jerusalem, his mother, Mary, being an ardent follower of Jesus. It was to her home that Peter fled when freed from jail (Acts 12:12). Many services were held here, and Mark as a young man must have been greatly impressed by the church leaders who visited his family. Undoubtedly he came to know the Disciples of

Jesus, and, though ten or fifteen years younger, was moved to commit his life to Christian service. He was also deeply affected by the piety, culture and modest luxury of his family.

His actual ministry began under Barnabas and Paul. While on a missionary journey to Cyprus, he and Paul differed so strongly that they felt it wise to separate. However, he and Barnabas continued to be closely associated. Several years later Mark and Paul were reconciled, and his former teacher recommended him to the Colossian church (Colossians 4:10).

Mark must have been about twenty at the time of the crucifixion, and so he could have been an eye-witness. In fact the young man to whom Mark refers in Chapter fourteen is considered by some to be the writer himself. This reference to the youth who accompanied Jesus into the Garden of Gethsemane, might have been a personal experience of the author, and could account for these passages not being found in the other Gospels.

Although the above is scholarly conjecture, there is plenty of evidence to give it basis in fact. If so, Mark not only wrote from the knowledge he acquired from the Apostles about Jesus, but also from his own personal contact with the Master. Of one thing we are certain: regardless of whether he knew Jesus personally, there is unanimous agreement in tradition and among scholars that Mark was directly associated with the Apostles and was Peter's secretary.

Date

Mark may have completed his writings about the time of Peter's death (A.D. 65 to 70), for he had personally recorded Peter's words about Jesus' life and teachings. Eusebius, (A.D. 264-340) mentions the early Church Father Papias (A.D. 115) as crediting Mark with so reporting Peter's activity. Allowing that Mark was with Peter near the end, we may assume the completion of the Gospel to be about A.D. 70. That Mark predicts the fall of Jerusalem (Mark 13:2) which occurred in A.D. 70, leads many conservative Christian scholars to date this book after A.D. 50 and before A.D. 70. Recent writers contend for dates between A.D. 64 and 85.

THE GOSPEL ACCORDING TO LUKE

LUKE opens his Gospel by stating his intention of giving an accurate account of Christ's life and ministry. For a time this statement led to a great deal of controversy concerning his reliability as an historian. The primary criticism has to do with Luke's reference to Quirinius, Governor of Syria, and the Census (2:1-3) taken during Herod's administration. Herod died B.C. 4, and no census had been taken in Judea until A.D. 6-7. But Quirinius did not become governor until after Herod's death, which means that no census had occurred during Herod's rule.

A careful reading of Luke discloses the fact that he speaks of an *enrollment,* not a census. Recent research confirms that such an enrollment actually occurred at this time, a custom instituted by Emperor Augustus, and affecting Judea. Enrollment papers have been discovered dating back to A.D. 20, disclosing that such records were made of the population every 14 years. This would establish the possibility of a census in the years A.D. 6 and B.C. 8. Allowing a differential of two years in the process of executing the emperor's orders, an enrollment could have occurred in the year of Christ's birth, B.C. 6. Hence, Luke could be right regarding Herod and the enrollment, and partially wrong in reference to Governor Quirinius.

Extensive study by scholars shows Luke to be more

concerned with "history" than were the other Gospel writers. He compares favorably with the best historians of his time, though he is more interested in inner history than in outer events. But none were historians in our modern sense, for critical analysis and documentation as we know it today began only about 150 years ago.

Content

In the book of Luke, the preface, and the stories regarding the birth and childhood of Jesus are distinctly different from those found in Matthew and Mark. The first two chapters include the prophecy to Elizabeth and Mary of Jesus' birth, the birth of John the Baptist and Jesus, as well as a brief account of the childhood of the Master.

The third chapter opens with an account of John's ministry which culminates in the baptism of Jesus (3:21). Luke then confirms the importance of this occasion and of Christ's ministry by a genealogical analysis of Jesus' forebears, a conclusive proof to Luke of his messiahship.

The fourth chapter concerns the Temptation in the Wilderness and Christ's commitment to his call and ministry. From here he returns to Galilee to bear witness of his faith: "And He taught in their Synagogues, being glorified by all" (4:15). This commitment is climaxed when Jesus returns to his home town synagogue and reads from Isaiah, "The spirit of the Lord is upon me, because he has anointed me to preach good news to the poor" (Luke 4:16-19 and Isaiah 61:1-2). Then follows the Sermon in Nazareth as well as some biographical material which is also found in Matthew and Mark. We are told of Christ's power, his enlistment of leaders and his compassion: "When the days drew near for him to be received up, he set his face to go to Jerusalem" (Luke 9:51).

Beginning at this point in the ninth chapter and continuing through a large part of the eighteenth, we discover material that is almost entirely Lukan. Here we learn of the parables of the Good Samaritan, the Rich Fool, the Marriage Feast, the Great Supper, the Lost Coin, the Prodigal Son, the Unjust Steward, the Rich Man and Lazarus, and the Pharisee and the Publican. Christ's mission, and the deep concern he feels, not only for his own people, but more particularly for the Gentiles, is obvious in these stories.

Then follow, from 18:31 to the end of the Gospel, the Lord's Passion and Resurrection. The account now parallels the writings of Matthew and Mark, particularly when Luke deals with Zacchaeus, the Penitent Robber and the incident on the Road to Emmaus. Luke, however, enlarges upon the words of Mark regarding the Passion and the Resurrection. He evidently draws upon other sources, giving way to a richer description of these events.

Author

We cannot deal with the Gospel of Luke without including Acts of the Apostles, because the style pattern and certain other evidence clearly point to a common authorship of these volumes.

In both books the writer addresses himself to a man named Theophilus. He also writes in Acts: "In the first book, O Theophilus, I have dealt with all that Jesus began to do and teach" (Acts 1:1). This is an obvious reference to the Gospel of Luke.

Vocabulary, style and emphasis in Luke bind it with Acts. For example, the narratives dealing with the resurrection and the forty day teaching ministry of Jesus show amazing similarity. Scholars now agree that what we have here is common authorship of a two-volume work, Luke-Acts.

Luke was a Gentile physician from Antioch of Syria. He probably converted to Christianity fifteen or twenty years after Christ's death. He was unquestionably well educated as evidenced in the refined literary nature of his writings. The fact that he was a physician (Colossians 4:14) would further corroborate his cultural training and education. His use of medical terms (Luke 8:43) as well as his doctor's perspective certainly support the fact that he was "the beloved physician." To all this, we can add the claims of tradition. Justin Martyr, Tatian and Marcion held to the Lukan authorship. Tertullian continually quoted Luke's writings with no indication of doubt regarding Luke as the author, which is not necessarily proof but is very strong support of modern scholarly analysis and opinion.

Luke places events in an order similar to those of the other Synoptics, Matthew and Mark, although his other sources are harder to identify. Luke 1:1-4 indicates there were both oral and written narrative materials available to him, who, though not an eyewitness himself, had access to those who had seen the Lord. It is generally believed that Mark and the so-called "Petrine Tradition" were major sources of such written material. Scholars further suppose that another document, the "Logia" or words of Jesus, may have been accessible to Luke—a document which is not extant.

Furthermore, Luke being a close companion of Paul was able, not only to put his hand on written materials, but was undoubtedly flooded with all kinds of oral reports. His two years in Caesaria (Acts 24:27) surely put him in touch with invaluable facts concerning the life of Christ and the Apostles.

Quite likely Mary, the mother of Jesus, was alive at this time, A.D. 57, and if so, Luke may have met her. Mary would have been an unusually reliable witness to the truth of the growing tradition regarding her son. Add to this, Luke's visits to Palestine and Rome, where he would have met several of the Twelve, and one can begin to understand the authoritative manner in which he writes.

The more we study Luke's writings, both the Gospel and Acts, the more we sense that his knowledge of Christ and the Apostles was cumulative, going back over a long period of time and gathered from an extensive association with those who had been personal friends.

Date

We know nothing about this Greek-speaking Gentile until his meeting with Paul at Troas about A.D. 51. At that time Luke was already an active preacher and missionary of note. Authorities date the writing of his two-volume history somewhere in the period between A.D. 60 and the closing year of Emperor Domitian's reign A.D. 96.

Writers of the Second Century knew this Gospel well. As early as A.D. 150 Justin Martin writes of details to be found only in Luke, while his pupil Tatian included such information in his Diatessaron. The earliest date would be around A.D. 60, the latest about A.D. 90. The one major clue from the author himself is to be found in Luke's reference to Jerusalem being surrounded by armies (Luke 21:20), which would indicate the impending destruction of the city. Thus we could narrow down the time of the writing of Luke's Gospel to the years A.D. 70-90.

THE GOSPEL ACCORDING TO JOHN

THERE is something contemporary about John's Gospel, especially regarding the judgment of God and the resurrected life of the believer. He speaks of both as present spiritual experiences, while the other evangelists see them mainly as future and final ("eschatological") events.

Content

The Fourth Gospel is unusually strong in doctrinal questions and in theological argument, being comparable to Paul's writings in such matters. To this we should add that the author had a flair for dates, places and names. He is not the story teller that Mark and Luke were, as he was less interested in biography than in ideas. John gives emphasis to those aspects of the Master's life that establish faith and understanding. Jesus is the "Word" become flesh.

John does not refer to Christ's birth, his childhood or even his baptism. Neither does he mention the Temptation in the Wilderness. His only comment about John the Baptist is a doctrinal statement which ignores the historic circumstances entirely. There is likewise no reference to the Transfiguration, the Agony in the Garden or the institution of the Lord's Supper. He also omits many of the miracles and does not include any of the parables. The author uses incidents in

Christ's life only when such events offer obvious possibilities of spiritual interpretation and evaluation. It becomes evident that many incidents of religious importance to Mark and Luke were evidently of no such weighty value to John.

Christ's active ministry in the Synoptics appears to span a year's time; John extends this period over three years. The first three Gospels leave the impression that Jesus' ministry was primarily spent in Galilee, while the Fourth Gospel makes little of this geographical area.

On the other hand, there are striking additions in John's Gospel, such as the changing of water into wine, the ceremony of foot-washing and the raising of Lazarus. Further study would show other variations from the Synoptics, but it is sufficient to keep in mind that John wrote from a different point of view and from other sources than the Synoptics, although there is every evidence that he was familiar with them, especially with Mark's material. He gives us a refreshing picture of Christ's life, one that many people consider the most inspiring of the four Gospels.

Message

John develops a richer doctrine of Jesus Christ ("Christology") than the other three authors. This fact is probably the result of his writing after Paul's death, at a time when the church had acquired growing strength and leadership. This, of course, could account for a more organized theology about Jesus. John emphasizes God as being in Christ or Christ as the Son of the Living God. Jesus becomes "the Logos," God's Word incarnate.

The Jesus of the Synoptics hesitates to speak of himself in messianic terms, cautioning his followers not to mention their cures or other amazing acts they had witnessed. But John presents Jesus as being anxious to assert his supernatural being, thus proclaiming his divinity. It is quite evident that John is primarily interested in convincing the reader that Jesus is the Son of God (John 20:31), something more than a historical personality. Jesus is the Christ, God become flesh. And all of this is God's plan from the beginning of creation.

Author

The twenty-first chapter of the Fourth Gospel states frankly that "the beloved disciple" is the author. Many modern scholars, however, consider this chapter to have been added by one who wanted to support the authenticity of John the Apostle's authorship. There is nothing reprehensible about this, for such a procedure was not unusual in ancient times. Such a redactor (as these men are called) was hoping to add merit to the book by vouching for its apostolic source.

John the Apostle, son of Zebedee, has generally been considered the author of the four books by his name as well as the book of Revelation. But between 1800 and 1820 a serious debate arose regarding the Johannine writings which continues until this day. The three theories of authorship revolve about John, son of Zebedee, John the Elder of Ephesus, and an unknown young man of Jerusalem. Whether one or more of these three is involved in creating these writings is not of vital importance. The content and significance of the books are the pertinent matter.

It is interesting to note that the author of the Book of John contends that he was an eye-witness of the crucifixion. "He who saw it has borne witness—his testimony is true, and he knows that he tells the truth—that you also may believe" (John 19:35). This being so, and if John the Apostle was sixteen or seventeen at the time he first joined the band of disciples, then he could have lived to a ripe old age and have written the Gospel about A.D. 100. Tradition gives much support to this possibility.

A study of the manuscripts of the early Church Fathers only further confuses the issue. Such men as Irenaeus (A.D. 180), Papias (A.D. 140), and still another as early as A.D. 116, all write about a certain John author of the Gospel, but without specifically leaving us with proof of the Apostle's authorship.

One more consideration: It was not unusual in ancient times for an author to use an honored name to give emphasis to his writings, and this is another of the explanations offered by those who contend that John the Apostle was not the author. But here again we need to appraise the insights, the material itself, and the spiritual qualities, rather than authorship alone, to establish the worth of the Johannine works. Content is more important than authorship and truth more than a name. We would be remiss, however, if we fail to discuss the controversy regarding the human source of these books.

Date

We have written evidence that the Johannine writings were in existence at least by the middle of the second century. They had probably been in circulation for some time. Careful reading discloses that the author knew Luke's Gospel, which was written about A.D. 70-90. With these facts at hand, scholars quite generally assume the Gospel of John and his three Letters to have been written about A.D. 100.

ACTS OF THE APOSTLES

OTHER than the Gospels, the Book of Acts is our finest revelation of God as seen in Jesus. We owe an eternal debt of gratitude to this wonderful physician and preacher of the Early Church whose writings are masterpieces of clarity and beauty. But even more significant, Luke has enriched all Christendom by his magnificent faith in the Gospel of Christ and in his recording of church history.

Content

Acts of the Apostles is the first history we have of the Church. In fact, it is the only history of the first century Christian Community. Though the title would indicate that the author writes of the Apostles in general, the fact is that it concerns primarily the Disciple Peter and the Missionary Paul. John is also mentioned briefly, along with Stephen, the first martyr (6:5); Philip, an evangelist to the Gentiles (8:5); Barnabas, Paul's companion and a missionary to the Greeks (11:22); and James, brother of Jesus, who became leader of the Jerusalem Church (12:17; 15:13; 21:18). But for all practical purposes the Book of Acts is the story of Peter and Paul.

The Book of Acts can be divided into two sections. The first half consists of material collected by the author from the many sources which must have been readily available to the leaders of the Early Church. He writes as a compiler. In the second half, beginning in the sixteenth chapter, Luke writes as an observer and as a participant using the first person plural, indicating that he is an eyewitness. These passages are often referred to as the "We" sections.

It is obvious that Luke is describing the process and development of a small provincial church into a world wide community of Christians—first the Jerusalem Christians, then the Hellenists, and later the complete divorcement of the Christian community from the Jewish nation. The Christian Church is born.

Luke has written his history in six divisions The first five chapters concern the Jerusalem congregations. From six through a large part of chapter nine, we are given the outreach of the faith into Palestine. In chapters nine through twelve Christ's Gospel spreads from Palestine to Antioch in Syria, and in chapters twelve through fifteen from Syria to Asia Minor. Paul's work in Europe is spelled out in chapters sixteen to nineteen. Finally, in Chapters twenty to twenty-eight, we are told of Paul's last days. We can sum up the contents of Acts by saying it is a history of the Christian Church from the time it was primarily a Jewish sect until it grew into a universal institution in the Hellenistic (late Mediterranean) civilization.

Message

Luke is explaining to Theophilus the story of the Church's birth and growth as it now becomes a religion for the world. In so doing he braces the Christians in their conflict with the Roman Empire by strengthening their faith in Jesus Christ, the Messiah.

Luke brings home his message by a series of brief sermons, probably condensed and in his own words, all of them essentially the Apostolic Gospel. There is one God,

Creator of heaven and earth, revealed in Jesus, the Christ, who is now his final messenger and Redeemer. Salvation and judgment are to be had in his name as a fulfillment of Jewish Scripture. It is the story of what Christ, the Son of God, has done for man. God is acting personally through Jesus in history.

In Acts, Luke personalizes his relationship with the events he participated in by using the personal pronoun "We." We find in Acts 16:11 that Luke is travelling with Paul from Troas to Philippi, where mention is made of Paul's arrest and imprisonment. At this point he ceases to use "we," indicating that the author was not incarcerated with his companion at Philippi (16:16, 19-34). But later on, when Paul finally returns to Macedonia, Luke again writes in the first person plural, and so continues to the end of the book.

Such a close association with Paul and his travels preeminently equipped the author to write of the Early Church and the great missioner's journeys.

The fact that Luke wrote his Gospel and Acts is evidence that he was dissatisfied with the fragmentary, perhaps garbled, accounts available to him at the time. The folk lore and stories were therefore edited by him to make what he considered to be a more reliable and authoritative account (Luke 1:2) of Christ's life and the beginnings of the Christian Church.

The Author—St. Luke

See page 193

The Date—A.D. 70-90.

See page 195

THE LETTER OF PAUL TO THE ROMANS

PAUL is uniquely practical. He knows how to relate theological theory and abstract thought to the everyday activities of men. It is in Paul that we find much of our Christian theology delineated. The Letter to the Romans is his most systematic theological statement.

Content

This epistle is roughly divided into two sections: Chapters one through eleven dealing with doctrinal aspects of the faith; the remaining five chapters with the practical application of religion.

Paul sees man as a sinner whose salvation and deliverance is to be found in Christ (Chapters 1-8). More specifically: The law alone is powerless to conquer the flesh, the creaturedom of man. Man's hope rests, not in good works, important as they are, but in faith which alone secures him. His faith in Christ is essential to justification. The baptism of the Christian is the seal and ultimate expression of man's union with Christ, and in faith through Christ with God. Then man becomes possessed of the spirit. Chapter eight is the climax of this theme and, along with the thirteenth chapter of 1 Corinthians, is one of the greatest inspirational sections in the New Testament.

Chapters nine through eleven concern the fate of the Jewish people whose rejection of Christ as the Messiah is a source of considerable anguish to Paul, who, as a former enthusiastic Pharisee, was as critical of Jesus as his earlier colleagues.

Paul explores predestination in chapter nine. This idea of man's destiny is woven into the fabric of his remarks about his people's rejection of Jesus. Moving on into the tenth chapter, we are reminded of man's free will and the hope of salvation as an act of faith, a choice available to all men. Finally, in the eleventh chapter Paul stresses mediation and reconciliation made possible through the mercies of God.

The latter part of the Letter, chapters twelve through sixteen, is a practical exposition of Christian teaching in relationship to contemporary problems facing members of the church in Rome. The Christian should not only love and serve his own, but should be thoughtful toward his persecutors, blessing, not cursing them.

The thirteenth chapter emphasizes the necessity and responsibility of good citizens to obey the constituted authorities, pointing out that civil authority indirectly comes from God and therefore exists for the general welfare of all. Roman political power is seen, not as an evil, but as a necessity. This chapter concludes with advice to obey the biblical commandments which under the new dispensation are the spiritual fruits of Christian love.

Evidently Paul felt it necessary in the fourteenth chapter to write concerning such matters as vegetarianism and sabbatarianism. There were members who emphasized exterior disciplines at the expense of inner spiritual values. Paul put it concisely when he writes, "He who observes the day, observes it in honor of the Lord." And, "He also who eats, eats in honor of the Lord. . . ." (Romans 14:6). The important matter is to keep one's faith in God, "For the kingdom of

God does not mean food and drink but righteousness and peace and joy in the Holy Spirit."

The closing two chapters are concerned with the author's personal plans, his desire for the prayers of his followers, after which come greetings and the benediction. He stresses his tremendous indebtedness to Christ for the gospel and the obligation to preach the word of righteousness. Before closing the Epistle he reminds them of dissenters and trouble makers and suggests they avoid them, bearing witness of their faith, awaiting the time when "the God of peace will . . . crush Satan under (their) feet" (Romans 16:20).

Message

To understand the Bible one should seek out the basic insights and abiding values rather than become lost in details. Paul, as other authors of his day, wrote for his contemporaries, and cultural differences make it sometimes difficult for us to understand him without adequate commentaries. His writings live, however, because of certain basic truths which transcend time and environment. This characteristic is particularly true of his Letter to the Romans.

The heart of this letter is God's righteousness touching human experience and fulfilling the urgent spiritual need of man to be at one with God. Man's response to God's concern is realized in Christ, whose love, coupled to man's faith, makes salvation possible.

No other New Testament book has been as fruitful in theological content as Romans. In fact, most of the basic theological vocabulary is rooted in this letter: adoption, justification, and sanctification are only a few of the words providing meaning to Christian thought.

Man is condemned as a rebellious creature, and his redemption requires that he be given a legal as well as a personal vindication, that he be clothed in spiritual righteousness. This salvation cannot be earned, nor this righteousness be realized in fact, but must be accepted in faith. Christ propitiates, through the sacrifice of his life, this alienation of man from God, thus restoring man to a place in God's kingdom. Both personally and racially man is dependent upon this grace which is in Christ.

The question now arises: Has this teaching of salvation by faith eliminated the covenant of the law with Israel? As God has chosen Israel as the vehicle of revelation, so now he speaks to the Gentile. This new law of love, and the faith that releases it, is not a denial but a fulfillment of the old law.

In the last few chapters Paul moves from a theological approach to salvation to certain practical applications of ethics. The Christian is not excused from moral obligation but is impelled to live a righteous life: "Let love be genuine; hate what is evil, hold fast to what is good. . . ." (12:9).

Thus Paul ties together theological theory with a practical application. In Romans he proves himself a missionary, preacher and theologian, a rare combination in any age.

It is evident that Paul is preparing the Roman Christians for his visit. At least this is the incidental reason for his writing them. However, the epistle is extraordinarily long, indicating Paul had other purposes in mind. As we read on we discover that he is anxious that the church in Rome profit by the experiences of Christ's followers elsewhere, perhaps in Corinth and Galatia, and that unnecessary controversy thus be avoided.

There is also the feeling that Paul, being proud of his Roman citizenship, wants the Roman church to bear a particularly strong witness. Even as early as the middle of the first century Paul is aware of the influence and the strategic importance of the Eternal City to the Christian faith, a significance which history has since vindicated.

Author

Most scholars agree that Paul is the author of thirteen of the New Testaments Letters. There were other writings from his pen, some of which are referred to in Second Thessalonians 3:17 and in First Corinthians 5:9, but these were either lost, destroyed in full or part, or were not considered of canonical worth. Although Paul's missionary work must have necessitated a great deal of speaking, his major forte was letter writing. At least, the evidence of the centuries demonstrates the power of his pen.

His Jewish name was Saul, and being of the tribe of Benjamin, he might possibly have been named after the famous king of that tribe, renowned in the annals of Israel. Like many Jews who were Roman citizens, he also bore the Roman version of the name which was Paul, and excepting in the first part of Acts, he is always referred to by this name. Undoubtedly this proved helpful during his travels through the Empire.

He was born in Tarsus, a famous University town and capital of Cilicia. As a full citizen of Tarsus, he was eligible for all the civil rights granted a Roman. Furthermore, he was freeborn, which meant that his family, perhaps a generation or so back, had been awarded citizenship as a special recognition of service. Paul was proud of this freeborn citizenship and refers to it in Acts 22:28.

On several occasions Paul used his privileged status as a Roman to avoid mistreatment at the hands of the authorities as in Philippi and Jerusalem. There is no question about it, Paul's Roman citizenship strengthened him in his preaching to the Gentiles and protected him from overzealous officials in the Roman colonies.

But Paul was also a loyal Jew and justly proud of his background and training. His early education was in Tarsus where he was strongly affected by the Stoics. Later, however, he studied at Jerusalem under the great Pharisee Gamaliel, whose liberality stood in sharp contrast to Paul's fanatical hatred of the Christian sect. It seems strange that he should have shown such bigotry having been taught by such a tolerant and understanding teacher.

Paul spoke Aramaic fluently which indicated a strong Hebraic background. This, as well as his writings, indicate that he was a Pharisee of Pharisees and that his family brought him up in the ethnic and cultural background of Jewry and not simply as a Greek-speaking citizen of Tarsus.

His one ambition was to be faithful to the traditions of his people, to fulfill the faith of his fathers. But he was overzealous and blindly expressed his youthful enthusiasm by persecuting the heretical followers of Jesus. In Acts 7:58 to 8:1 we find him sanctioning the stoning of Stephen, the first Christian martyr. Stirred to heated fanaticism by this event, he seeks authority from the high priest to go to Damascus and arrest the disciples of Jesus, to bind them in chains and bring them to Jerusalem.

It is en route to Damascus that a traumatic experience occurs. A great light flashes before him and Jesus appears to him, speaking clearly and explicitly: "Saul, Saul, why persecutest thou me." Blinded by the light, he is brought to Damascus where Ananias baptizes him, after which he goes directly to the Synagogues of the city to confess Christ as Lord and Master of his life. This theophany accounts for a complete reversal in Paul's life. From now on he becomes the great missioner of the early Church. Whereas he was a Pharisee among Pharisees, now he is a Christian among Christians.

Paul was self-supporting whenever there was danger of his being accused of commercialism. He never compromised his message by asking for money for himself and his entourage. He was a tent-maker by trade, having been given a training in this occupation by his family. This early Jewish custom of instructing children, not only to think clearly, but also to do manual work, stood Paul in good stead. He was able to earn his bread by the labor of his hands, while at the same time he gave his heart and mind to preaching the Gospel.

Format of Paul's Letters

Paul's Epistles were not open letters for general publication. They were written specifically to individuals or churches and contained advice and counsel directed to specific addressees.

His letters were dictated, but he often finished a letter with a note in his own handwriting to add weight and warmth to it.

There is a formula common to all his correspondence. He first names himself or himself and associates. Then follow references to the recipients in the city and/or the region involved, followed by a few words concerning their Christian condition. The salutation is next in order and calls upon the "grace and peace" of God and Christ. Now comes a note of thanksgiving for God's mercies to the author or/and the church to which he writes. The only exception to this is found in his Letter to the Galatians, churches in which he finds no reason for thanksgiving.

There is less of a pattern seen in his closings and yet here, too, certain formalities are evident. Where he knows the church people well, he avoids the diplomatic error of personally referring to particular individuals, but in his Letters to the Romans and Colossians, churches he had yet to visit, he mentions specific individuals. In all cases, however, he extends greetings from his companions. The inevitable conclusion to an epistle is a Pauline benediction, "The grace of our Lord Jesus Christ be with you."

It is well to understand why some minor parts of Paul's

letters are not clear to the contemporary reader. After all, they are *personal* letters directed to people who were familiar with problems currently involving them. We therefore have to interpret these situations by reading between the lines. But by and large Paul's epistles are unusually clear to the modern reader.

The general pattern of content was first, a treatise regarding doctrinal matters or questions, afterwards he deals with practical problems, encouraging the people to exemplify their faith in moral behavior. Such advice often concerned the church directly, while at other times Paul speaks to all Christians in general.

It must at times confuse the layman when he discovers Paul to be the primary source of some of the major theological differences that have stimulated, and at times plagued, the church over the centuries. Certainly Paul was not writing dogmatic theology as such and would be every bit as surprised as the average modern reader that so much quibbling has sprung from his pastoral correspondence. He never expected his Letters to be anything more than what he intended them to be—contemporary communications to a contemporary people. Of one thing there can be no equivocation: Paul saw the Christian faith rooted in Jesus Christ ("the Messiah"), God made flesh.

Paul's letters are the earliest extant Christian writings. Though scholars are uncertain as to the exact sequence, they are fairly confident that the Letters to the Thessalonians and Galatians were the first. The Pauline writings can probably be dated between the years A.D. 50-68, his martyrdom occurring about A.D. 68.

Date

Paul returned to Corinth after completing his third missionary journey. From what we can piece together from Acts regarding his activities, he probably wrote to the Romans about this time. We also know from the opening salutation that Timothy is with him in Corinth, sharing his three-month sojourn there.

Putting together a chronology of Paul's trips and activities leads us to believe that the Letter to the Romans was written about A.D. 55-56.

THE FIRST LETTER OF PAUL TO THE CORINTHIANS

FIRST and Second Corinthians appear to contain two letters, plus the fragments of two others which Paul wrote to the Corinthian Church. What we call First Corinthians is probably the second letter. In this epistle Paul pictures some of the moral and spiritual problems confronting this new church in an alien environment.

Another fact worth noting is that the account of the Lord's Supper is the oldest recorded in the New Testament.

Content

It is evident that the author is responding to the report of Chloe's people and the questions put to him by the Corinthian constituency. The outline of the letter is consequently an orderly and spirited discourse regarding these matters.

We begin with the usual salutation followed by six chapters concerning the divisions within the church, the nature and correctness of Paul's ministry, a barbed criticism of pagan immorality within the fellowship, and the unwarranted use of pagan courts to settle problems between members. Finally, he confronts them with the moral demands of Christian behavior in contrast to the sensual libertinism in their lives.

The last ten chapters are Paul's answers to the questions put to him by the Corinthian members.

He speaks of marriage in the light of the impending end of things, recommending the single life as the blessed one. However, marriage is a worthy state and to be commended: "I say this by way of concession, not of command" (1 Corinthians 7:6).

Chapters eight, nine, and ten are made up of homilies on things sacrificed to idols. He recognizes the transitional difficulties confronting the pagan who has converted to Christianity. He evaluates the meaning of idols and their meaninglessness to the Christian, yet he wisely recognizes the former pagan's problem in disassociating himself from idolatry, and the sense of sin which overcomes him when he eats food which has been offered to idols. "Therefore, if (such) food is a cause of my brother's falling, I will never eat meat, lest I cause my brother to fall" (1 Corinthians 8:13).

The next chapter is an excellent treatment of spiritual freedom, especially in relationship to the above problem of idols. The tenth chapter follows through with an evaluation of idolatry as it effects the true worship of God and man's social responsibility to his neighbor.

Then comes a section on good manners in worship: A woman's head should be covered, a man's uncovered when worshipping. At the Lord's supper the members should be considerate toward one another, not humiliating those who have nothing or acting in an intemperate manner. "Whoever, therefore, eats the bread or drinks the cup of the Lord in an unworthy manner will be guilty of profaning the body and blood of the Lord" (1 Corinthians 11:27).

Chapters twelve through fourteen make up a section dealing with the spiritual talents of the members. He speaks of many varieties of gifts, admonishing them to remember the common good, and, above all, their obligation to Christ.

A climax is reached in the thirteenth chapter where Paul writes of love as the greatest gift of all. Moving on into the fourteenth chapter he asks that they "Make love (their) aim," remembering that the unbeliever or outsider will find no meaning in "tongues" or "prophesy" unless he discovers "that God is really among you" (1 Corinthians 14:25).

In chapter fifteen the author expands the Christian concept of the resurrection of the body and Christ's relationship to this belief. Here we discover some of the most significant passages on the nature of man's immortality.

The final chapter offers a practical suggestion to the Corinthian Church regarding offerings and their disposition in Jerusalem. Then follow the usual Pauline greetings and closing.

Purpose

Paul is seeking to strengthen the Corinthian Church members so they will not succumb to the unrestrained and undisciplined moral behavior of their pagan neighbors.

He also seeks to give them a more respectful and disciplined attitude toward worship, especially regarding the most significant rite of the church, the Lord's Supper.

There is also disclosed his concern for unrestrained emotional indulgence typical of the Corinthian people. Although he recognizes their high regard for such ecstatic phenomena as "speaking in tongues," trances and visions, he reminds them that love and neighborly concern are paramount.

Finally, he seeks to clarify in their minds the doctrinal significance of the resurrection of the dead.

Perhaps the purpose of the letter can be put in this manner: It is a stern exposition, entreaty, and narration on Christian ideals, showing how Christian experience and concepts stand in conflict with the practices and sophistry of the pagan world—a conflict which still goes on in our day.

Author—St. Paul

See page 207

Date

Stephanas, Fortunatus, and Achaicus brought a letter to Paul, along with a contribution, from the church in Corinth. They were anxious that he clarify certain questions. Paul answered from Ephesus where he was preparing extensive plans for a long and important trip to Macedonia. However, he wrote of remaining in Ephesus until after Pentecost, indicating that the letter must have been written that same winter. Piecing together such information, it is reasonable to assume that this first letter was posted from Ephesus, the winter of A.D. 54 or 55 (Acts 24:17 and 1 Corinthians 16:5-8).

THE SECOND LETTER OF PAUL TO THE CORINTHIANS

THE spiritual inertia of some of the churches had grown intolerable. Desertion and criticism was altogether too prevalent. Paul in his letter firmly defends his stand and in so doing clarifies ethical and religious matters of great concern to the Early Church.

Content

Second Corinthians can be roughly divided into five sections, plus the personal introduction and the concluding salutation in Chapters One and Thirteen.

The first division, chapters one through six, is a personal discussion of Paul's past, particularly regarding his ministry in Corinth. Here he explains changes in his plans, and, after making certain personal comments, discusses the Christian ministry itself. It is an apologia, a strong defense of the ministry, his ministry.

In verses 2:14 through 4:6 he writes of the nature and poignancy of the ministry showing its power and sincerity (11 Cor. 2:14). From the early part of the fourth chapter to the eleventh verse of the fifth, he treats the difficulties, the aspirations, the hope and the rewards of the ministry (4:16). From here to the start of the seventh chapter he concerns himself with the objective, the foundation, the example, the fulfillment, and appeal of the ministry.

The second section, chapter 7:5 to 7:16 concerns the return of Titus to Macedonia and the good news he brought Paul from his friends in the Corinthian church regarding their esteem for him and Christ's word. He expresses pleasure at the effect of his first epistle.

Then follow Paul's comments about giving, especially the generosity of the poor churches of Macedonia. This third part of the letter, Chapters 8 through 9:15, exalts the value and the grace of giving and commends Titus to them as one commissioned to accept their love and generosity in stewardship. He is certain they will give willingly. "Now it is superfluous for me to write to you about the offering for the saints, for I know your readiness" (11 Corinthians 9:1).

The fourth part, chapters ten through 12:13, is a strong personal defense of Paul's Apostolic authority, a claim which he will not minimize. Indeed, he insists he possesses a superiority of Apostleship.

The last major section, chapters 12:14 through 13:10, deals with his anticipated visit to Corinth. He assures them that he will meet them all personally, not sparing any of those guilty of apostasy (11 Cor. 13:2).

The last verses of the letter are the usual Pauline greeting and benediction.

Purpose

Second Corinthians gives an excellent biographical picture of the great missioner, more so than any other of his writings. In it we see him as a firm and dedicated leader as well as a man of tender consideration and feeling.

It is evident that Paul intended in this letter to set the record straight regarding the many accusations made against him, not alone in Corinth, but in all the cities where he had preached. He had been particularly harassed in Galatia, and he did not intend to have matters get out of hand in Corinth.

Of one thing he insisted: Christ is head of the Church. All else is relatively insignificant. He bore witness to this before his accusers and insisted that the Church recognize Christ's authority and that the members stop their personal quibbling. When he had finished his highly personalized epistle, none could be in doubt as to where he stood and what were the basic responsibilities of a church member in good standing.

To be certain that the letter was something more than defensive, he saw to it that the Corinthians got their minds off themselves by insisting that they contribute to the poor of Jerusalem with the same enthusiasm and generosity as was shown by their fellow Christians in Achaia and Macedonia.

Paul may have been defending himself but not to the point of neglecting his responsibility to the Corinthian church. Above all he was a good minister of Jesus Christ and his major objective in this second letter was that they know the Lord as he had come to know him: "Mend your ways, heed my appeal, agree with one another, live in peace, and the God of love and peace will be with you" (II Corinthians 13:11).

Author—St. Paul

See page 207

Date

A great riot broke out in Ephesus shortly after Paul had written I Corinthians (Acts 19), possibly hastening his trip to Macedonia enroute to Corinth. Finally he met with

Titus who was returning from Corinth and who brought him up to date regarding conditions there. Although the first letter had helped, there was still dissension, especially concerning the genuineness of Paul's apostleship. Paul immediately dispatched Titus with the Second Letter to the Corinthians defending his ministry and reiterating much of what he had said in the first epistle. This second note was probably posted in the year A.D. 55 or 56.

THE LETTER OF PAUL TO THE GALATIANS

THIS letter is a brilliant affirmation of Christian freedom, actually an emancipation statement on the dangers of legalism in religion. It has been called "the Christian Declaration of Independence."

Content

The first ten verses of the letter are introductory. He briefly states his apostleship and salvation through Christ as the basis of spiritual freedom, challenging the Galatians to this same liberty which epitomizes the purpose of his letter.

In Chapters 1:11 through 2:21, the author strongly supports and vindicates his apostolic authority, which is evidenced by his commission from Christ, not man, and by the recognition given him by the Church authorities in Jerusalem.

He criticizes Peter's provincialism concerning the Gentile converts, opposing him for his over-emphasis upon the law and certain Jewish legalisms regarding food and circumcision: "I do not nullify the grace of God; for if justification were through the law, then Christ died to no purpose" (2:21).

Now follows a theological argument on the impotence of legalism as a way of redemption. This section, chapters four and five, is a challenging assertion of justification by faith. He speaks not only from his personal experience but refers to their own background wherein faith, rather than obedience to the law, had saved them. "Does he who supplies the Spirit . . . do so by works of the law, or by hearing with faith" (3:5).

He now cites the case of Abraham and how faith affected him. It should be self-evident that complete obedience to the law was impossible then or now and that Christ's coming redeemed man from the tyranny of the law.

However, he reminds the Galatians that the law is not "against the promises of God" (3:21), but a means of guiding men to Christ. Then he concludes with the argument that this freedom as sons of God, made liberty superior to law.

The next major division is in Chapters 5:1 through 6:10 and is a practical exposition on the effects of liberty. He deals first with the freedom of the Christian life expressed in loving service in contrast to legalism. This difference is symbolized in the struggle between the flesh and the spirit —works of the flesh, fruits of the Spirit. The social implication of this position is then concisely stated: "Bear one another's burdens, and so fulfill the law of Christ" (6:2).

The last few verses of the sixth chapter summarize the motive, price and suffering entailed in the doctrine of liberty. The last verse is the Pauline benediction.

Message

Here is a message to those who, having received a joyous conversion, are now quarrelling or are disturbed by teachers who have unsettled their faith by stressing the Jewish law and mores as necessary to the Christian experience.

Paul defends himself against his accusers, stressing the importance of freedom in Christ as man's way to salvation, rather than an entanglement "in a yoke of bondage." Christian liberty is not the liberty to sin but to be released to walk by the Spirit. The fruitage of this redemptive experience is love, joy, kindness, faithfulness and self-control. There can be no law against these, nor is there one that can produce them.

Author—St. Paul

See page 207

Date

There are many scholars who contend that this letter is the oldest of Paul's New Testament writings rather than his Epistles to the Thessalonians. They assume that Paul was writing to the churches he and Barnabas founded in Southern Galatia, probably penning his message from Antioch in Syria directly after the first missionary journey. If so, then this letter could be dated as early as A.D. 48. On the other hand, there are those who theorize that Paul wrote it from Ephesus, A.D. 52, about the time he was writing many of his other letters.

THE LETTER OF PAUL TO THE EPHESIANS

THIS letter is divided into two sections, the first doctrinal and the second hortatory. Though both are on the theme of the unity of the world in Christ, the first half is more particularly concerned with God's purpose as disclosed in the Christian witness, while the last half emphasizes the Church as an extension of the incarnation, the very body of Christ. It will be through the love and understanding of the faithful that unity will be brought about both in the Church and in the world—reconciliation will be in Christ.

Content

First we have the customary introduction and salutation (1:1-2) followed by a section, chapter one through three, disclosing God's purpose to unify all things in Christ.

We are instructed in the formation of the Church and man's gratitude for membership in Christ. Then follows a prayer that the Ephesians might understand their salvation, their inheritance, hope and power in Christ. The supremacy of Christ is firmly established.

The latter part of the first section concerns Paul's mission as an Apostle to the Gentiles, which mission is to reveal the Church as Christ's body and man's way into the fullness of God. Finally, there is a doxology, which is a concluding prayer to the doctrinal half of the letter.

The last half, chapters four through six deals with the conduct of the Church, emphasizing her importance as an instrument which reconciles all things in Christ.

Emphasis is given to the unity which is found in diversity. Paul points out that variety of human gifts and functions is an asset, not a hindrance to the faith.

At the same time, he reminds the Ephesians of the importance of moral standards, emphasizing the differences between pagan and Christian conduct. It is important, he exhorts them, to be worthy of their calling, and thus bear a corporate witness of behavior to the world about them.

He further proceeds to give guidance regarding Christian family relationships, stressing the value of mutual service and domestic standards between husband and wife, children and parents, master and slave.

Then follows a statement covering the conflict confronting the Church, a challenge to the members to be equipped with the armor of God and to do their part for the Church (6:10-17).

Finally, Paul adds a few personal comments and closes with a characteristic benediction.

Message

This letter is addressed to experienced church members in Ephesus who desire to enlarge their spiritual horizons and increase their knowledge.

Paul elaborates upon God's sovereignty, his purpose, and his intent for the Church. The divine plan of redemption is developed quite extensively in the first half of the letter.

In the second half he gives practical impetus to the doctrinal emphasis of the preceding section. He deals with Christian conduct specifically, pointing out that the Holy Spirit is the source of man's understanding of God, his very access to Him. In God we then discover truth, power, and unity.

Herein are the sources of life's meaning and the stimulus to spiritual joy.

In a very logical manner, the letter to the Ephesians leads man through an understanding of his redemption in Christ, the Holy Spirit, and the Father, into a practical application of faith in the everyday responsibilities of life.

Author—St. Paul

See page 207

Date

Possibly A.D. 60 or 61. The messenger who carried this letter was Tychicus who accompanied the slave Onesimus with a letter for Philemon. It is probable that he also carried several other of Paul's letters at this time.

THE LETTER OF PAUL TO THE PHILIPPIANS

THE Letter to the Philippians consists of two major emphases: first, the faith of the Christian as rooted in the Gospel, which is to "have righteousness, not based on the law, but through faith in Christ," the "righteousness from God that depends on faith. . . ." (3:9). The other emphasis is upon the joy which a Christian experiences in response to the message of Christ. Paul could also rejoice because he saw in the Philippians this testimony. He understood this contentment of spirit in spite of his impending imprisonment and execution.

Content

We outline the Letter as follows:

Philippians 1:1-11, consists of a salutation, expressions of Christian fellowship through thanksgiving, gratitude, and prayer.

Chapter 2:12-2:18: This portion deals with Paul's personal circumstances and his courage, a courage he coveted for the Philippians. Let them be worthy of the Gospel by following Christ, the exemplar of the faith, serving and obeying Him courageously.

In Chapter 2:19-2:30 Paul writes of his plan to send Timothy and Epaphroditus to them.

Chapter 3:1-4:4: Here we have a strong Pauline statement regarding the dangers of legalism, to which he adds a note about his own personal experiences. He goes on to exhort them to live harmoniously, avoiding the worldliness about them, striving always to be steadfast in Christ, for "our commonwealth is in heaven, and from it we await a Savior, the Lord Jesus Christ". . . . (3:20).

Chapter 4:4 to 4:23 contains advice and the usual greetings so typical of his letters. He goes on to express his joy in their unity and thoughtfulness, and concludes with the customary salutation.

Message

Paul excels in personalizing faith. He writes from a rich experience that supports his doctrinal teaching. His Letter to the Philippians is an exceptionally fine illustration of teaching truth by personalizing the evidence. Paul writes as one who has lived his faith. Paul tells of the risen Christ whose extraordinary powers and grace have affected him.

Though he emphasizes the importance of virtuous living, he goes on to speak of the joy that is founded in the risen Christ, who by his earthly suffering and death, glorifies righteousness with a price that gives to the Christian a spiritual motivation, unequaled by pagan faiths.

Author—St. Paul

See page 207

Date

The Letter to the Philippians was written near the end of Paul's imprisonment in Rome, which would date it about A.D. 56 or 57 to A.D. 60 or 61. We need to state here that several of the prison letters are thought by some to have been written from a prison in Caesarea, if so, this letter could have been composed as early as A.D. 55.

THE LETTER OF PAUL TO THE COLOSSIANS

THIS brief note from Paul's pen is another of his epistles of caution, admonition, and advice. Paul is ever mindful of the temptations of the pagan environment and its effect upon the Church. He exhorts the Christian community to stand by its Lord and Master, Jesus Christ.

Content

The opening chapter plus the first seven verses of the second concern the author's prayers for the Colossians and his appeal to them that they be true to the person of Christ who has come to man in the image of God. He is quite personal in his testimony at this point concerning his own call and suffering for the Church.

The second chapter reveals Christ as the source of doctrine, and challenges the false philosophies threatening the integrity of the faith. Let there be no compromise: Christ is the Godhead.

The third section, Chapters 3:5 through 4:6, is an ethical application of doctrine to every day living between Christians, husbands and wives, children and fathers, slaves and masters, as well as their contacts with the world.

He ends the epistle with certain personal matters and a final greeting. He speaks of an impending visit to Colossae from Mark with whom he has become reconciled; he extends greetings from Luke and Demas; and a suggestion that the Colossians exchange letters with the Church at Laodicea; and finally he pens a word regarding Archippus, their new minister.

Purpose

The theme of this letter is the pre-eminence of Christ. After two verses of salutation Paul begins his reply to the report brought to him by Epaphras regarding conditions in Colossae. The Christians there were troubled by false teachings which the Apostle sets about to correct by establishing a proper understanding of Jesus Christ.

The old religions were dying and new ones were being born. This condition led to the rise of many different sects which attempted to combine various concepts characteristic of the traditional faiths. The Early Church consequently found itself being diluted and altered by similar variants. This situation disturbed Paul who seeks in his letter to re-establish the basic theology about Christ.

Author—St. Paul

See page 207

Date

Colossians and Philemon were evidently mailed at the same time, being carried by the same messengers, Tychicus and Onesimus the slave who was returning to his master, Philemon. Hence, the dates A.D. 56 or 57 to A.D. 60 or 61.

THE FIRST LETTER OF PAUL TO THE THESSALONIANS

FIRST and Second Thessalonians are excellent examples of early missionary preaching. Though they lack a strong theological emphasis, they bear witness of the Gospel in clear and simple terms; salvation through Christ.

Content

The first chapter is basically concerned with the nature, qualifications, and character of the Church in Thessalonica.

Chapters two and three deal with Paul's apostolic contact and understanding with the church. He refers to his own personal relationship with them and their acceptance of him. This relationship is confirmed by his expression of concern and his continuing prayers for them.

In the remaining two chapters he deals with the serious sex problems prevalent in the Gentile communities and the need of discipline and restraint. In fact, matters of social conduct are treated in a most serious manner.

Then follows a discussion of the condition of the dead and their resurrection to life upon Christ's return, reminding the Thessalonians that the time of that occurrence will be unknown even to the righteous, "the day of the Lord will come like a thief in the night" (5:2). Finally come the customary greeting and exhortations.

Message

Paul is writing to the church in Thessalonica in response to Timothy's report of his recent visit there. The young disciple had come directly to Corinth that he might give first hand information to Paul. The report was evidently most encouraging, because a large part of the letter consists of praise and thanksgiving for the love and faith displayed by these people.

Paul's love of the Thessalonians finds expression in his longing to see them, but such sentiment does not eliminate his concern for their spiritual direction and welfare. He continues to appeal and exhort them to remain steadfast in their faith.

He particularly warns of the impurity of the Gentile world and the necessity of an inner discipline for their lives.

The author also admonishes them regarding certain errors and conflicts of opinion which had developed among them. But by and large there is little of the usual Pauline doctrinal emphasis, the epistle being largely personal in tone rather than theological. In many ways this is the most intimate of all his writings.

Paul assures his readers that God will avenge their persecutors, the "day of the Lord" will surely come. He reminds them that the signs of Christ's coming will be preceded by renewed prayer, exhortation, and thanksgiving. The reference to Christ's return receive scant attention elsewhere in Paul's letters, unless we consider Galatians 5:5 as an allusion to this idea, "For through the Spirit, by faith, we wait for the hope of righteousness." We know, however, that this theme was typical of much of the early apostolic preaching. The Book of Acts certainly depicts Peter (3:20, 21) and

Paul (17:31) as convinced believers in the early return of Christ to judge the world. But it is in First Thessalonians where we find Paul specifically referring to this controversial belief.

There are still large bodies of Christians who retain this doctrinal belief in the Second Coming, but for the overwhelming majority of Christians, this is now quite secondary to the fact that Christ is where man's heart is opened to him. This was the faith of Paul and the disciples; this is the faith today.

Author—St. Paul

See page 207

Date

Both letters to the Thessalonians were written from Corinth about A.D. 51, possibly a few months apart. Many consider First Thessalonians the oldest book of the New Testament canon.

THE SECOND LETTER OF PAUL TO THE THESSALONIANS

THIS letter opens with the typical Pauline salutation: "Paul, Silvanus, and Timothy, to the church of the Thessalonians in God our Father and the Lord Jesus Christ: Grace to you and peace from God the Father and the Lord Jesus Christ."

The first chapter continues with a note of thanksgiving for their faithfulness and an assurance of strength in the face of persecution. Paul writes of their continued growth, the destruction of their persecutors, and the glorification of Christ in their lives. He ends the chapter with an assurance of his prayers.

The next chapter refers, as in the First Letter, to the "coming of our Lord Jesus Christ." Evidently Paul is worried by the consequences of this belief in the lives of some of the people. Perhaps his eloquence in 1 Thessalonians has led them to cease constructive activity in anticipation of the imminent arrival of Christ. He reminds them of the signs and conditions that will be evident before the Lord returns. They are to apply themselves to the immediate responsibilities at hand.

He predicts apostasy in the ranks of the church, but reminds them of his gratitude for their steadfastness in that God has especially chosen them for salvation. He finishes the chapter by calling upon God to grace their lives with eternal comfort.

In the third chapter Paul exhorts them to live their lives in accord with the tradition "received from us." He is asking that they work diligently and faithfully; that they shun idleness, and in every way show themselves constructive workers and not mere busybodies. "Have nothing to do with those who refuse to work quietly and responsibly," he writes, warning such members, not as enemies, but as brothers.

Then follow the usual salutation and benediction written in his own hand.

Purpose

One of the major purposes of this letter is to offset the misunderstanding created by the First Epistle concerning the Lord's return in the near future. Reports coming to him indicated fanatical irresponsibility on the part of many who had become indifferent to the present world and its needs. He wants them to get back in stride with life and to act sensibly toward their present obligations and work.

Author—St. Paul

See page 207

Date—About A.D. 51

See page 232

THE FIRST LETTER OF PAUL TO TIMOTHY

THERE are three of Paul's letters whose purpose is to counsel and advise his assistants in the "care of the church." First and Second Timothy and Titus, frequently called the Pastoral Epistles, are similar in language, ethical instruction, and religious indoctrination. It is obvious that they share a common author and were written about the same time.

Although Paul's authorship of these letters is seriously questioned by a number of scholars, the generally accepted view is that he wrote them. It would be futile to enter into a lengthy discussion of the historic, ecclesiastical and literary reasons for and against the Pauline authorship. It is sufficient to say there is a difference of opinion.

But for the moment let us accept Paul as the writer.

Timothy was a young man of about thirty when Paul appointed him pastor of the Church in Ephesus. "Let no one despise your youth" (4:12). Further reading of I and II Timothy indicates that Timothy was timid or shy and suffered a stomach ailment. Paul felt the young man needed strengthening, and his letters are intended to bolster his confidence in carrying out the tremendous responsibility given him.

Content

The First Letter begins with a salutation followed by an

introduction regarding the emergency at Ephesus caused by erroneous teachings of doctrine. He proceeds to instruct Timothy in the essentials of the faith and bears witness to him and the congregation of his personal experience as an Apostle of Christ.

Following this preamble (1:1-17), Paul officially commits Timothy to the task of leading his people. In Chapters 1:18 to 4:5, Paul writes of Timothy's responsibilities regarding certain church matters. He deals with the organization and life of the institution, beginning with an emphasis upon prayer and going on to such subjects as worship by women, the status of the bishop's life and office, and the responsibilities of deacons to live an exemplary life. As usual Paul admonishes the women to know their place and to manage their families well.

The fourth chapter opens another section of the outline, beginning with a few strong words concerning apostasy, especially in reference to food and marriage. "For everything created by God is good, and nothing is to be rejected if it is received with thanksgiving. . . ." (4:4).

The remaining section, chapters four, five and six, consists primarily of personal admonitions regarding individual conduct. These include the inter-relationship of groups regarding sex and age; the honor due and the responsibility of widows; the position and duties of elders as well as the relationship of the congregation to them; and the place and status of the bondslave. Then follows a condemnation of false teachers and avariciousness, along with a charge to Christians in general that they have a proper attitude toward wealth, not "to set their hopes on uncertain riches but on God who richly furnishes us with everything to enjoy" (6:17).

The closing two verses contain a challenging salutation, "O Timothy, guard what has been entrusted to you" (6:20), etc.

Purpose

Paul outlines the ground rules for Timothy as a preacher and pastor. He instructs the congregation in its relationship to both Timothy and himself. In a very forceful way, Paul shows to Timothy, and all young men aspiring to the ministry, the basic elements of pastoral conduct.

Author—St. Paul

See page 207

Date

There are two theories regarding Paul's imprisonment and death in Rome which in turn would affect the possible dates of this letter. The first is that he was imprisoned only once in the Imperial City.

The second is that he was released about A.D. 61 and imprisoned again about A.D. 64. During this interval he travelled to Spain and the Near East, stopping in Epheseus, Macedonia and Crete. The Church Father, Clement of Rome, writes of Paul visiting "the bounds of the West," which could only mean Spain, and consequently, would substantiate the idea that Paul was later imprisoned and executed.

This would suggest his possible martyrdom about A.D. 64-68, and that the Pastorals were written in this period.

THE SECOND LETTER OF PAUL TO TIMOTHY

THIS epistle reveals a church that is fighting for its life, hemmed in as it is by a decaying paganism and an immoral society. Paul as an older man is writing to Timothy as one who will succeed him as a church leader. In fact, II Timothy is Paul's last message before his execution in Rome.

Content

The opening verses are a salutation and thanksgiving.

Chapter 1:6-2:13 is a brief statement to Timothy about his work as a teacher, with references to precedents established in Paul's life which can be helpful to him. (1:13). Paul wisely includes advice on the importance of Timothy's own spiritual life, an indispensable asset in his ministry to others.

The remainder of the letter treats the importance of true doctrine and the dangers of apostasy; a prophecy of a time of moral retreat; the necessity of faith in the Scripture, and a hearty defense of the faith which is best expressed in a steadfast moral and spiritual life. Paul's last charge includes his farewell—made extremely meaningful by his imminent death—and a final witness to God's care: "The Lord will rescue me from every evil and save me for his heavenly kingdom. To him be the glory forever and ever, Amen" (4:18).

The conclusion is a greeting and benediction.

Purpose

Paul identifies himself with Timothy in a very intimate way. He is conveying to the younger man the spiritual duties which Paul's impending death will force him to relinquish. "Do not be ashamed then of testifying to our Lord, nor me his prisoner . . . who saved us and called us with a holy calling . . ." (1:8). He writes of "us" which indicates his deep feeling for Timothy and his continuing ministry through him. He wants to strengthen Timothy with the faith that has fortified him.

Paul's one basic answer to the dangers which beset the Church is a firm knowledge of the Scriptures. Paul wants Timothy to hold this light before the people.

The last few passages are a final challenge to Timothy, the pastor, to secure his strength in the Lord, truly good advice to ministers in any time or place. "But the Lord stood by me and gave me strength to proclaim the word fully . . ." (4:17).

Author—St. Paul

See page 207

Date—A.D. 61-68

See page 237

THE LETTER OF PAUL TO TITUS

CHRONOLOGICALLY this letter actually follows the First Letter to Timothy, although it follows the Second Letter in the New Testament.

The Church in Crete was poorly organized and in need of both spiritual and organizational guidance. Titus had been sent to the island to complete the establishment of the church and to strengthen the Cretans in their moral and ethical conduct.

Content

This letter is much like the other two Pastorals. Other than the greetings and salutations at the beginning and end, it is an appeal to establish a good church of faithful members, with Titus as the organizer, teacher and pastor.

Here are the basic matters discussed:

Chapter One has to do with administration, including such subjects as doctrine, the qualifications and appointment of elders, and the behavior of Christians when exposed to false teachers.

Chapter two relates to teaching the faith and its application to the members. Then follows advice regarding the behavior of older men and women; the duties of the younger set, and the relationship of slave and master. Titus is reminded, however, that the Gospel is not discriminatory: "For the grace of God has appeared for the salvation of all men . . ." (2:11).

The last chapter further defines Christian relationships, especially with the world at large. Paul is once more applying doctrine to the practical aspects of living day to day.

Purpose

The basic theme in the Letter to Titus is proper doctrine, especially in its practical application. Paul is always thorough in his indoctrination of his followers and in this epistle he wants to be sure that Titus not only improves the church organization in Crete, but that he instructs them soundly in theological and ethical matters.

Author—St. Paul

See page 207

Date—A.D. 61-68

See page 237

THE LETTER OF PAUL TO PHILEMON

PHILIPPIANS, Colossians, Ephesians and Philemon, the so-called Prison Epistles, were all composed while Paul was under house arrest in Rome. Though he was unable to travel, he was permitted to teach, write and have visitors. All of these letters refer to his bonds, and though a few scholars say they could have been penned from Caesarea, the general consensus is that the epistles were sent from the Imperial City. Some of Paul's most effective work was done while suffering incarceration.

Content

Philemon was an important business man of Colossae from whom Onesimus, his slave, had stolen property and money.

The slave had fled to Rome where he had come in contact with the Apostle, proving himself, not only a good convert but a very promising assistant to Paul.

This is the only private letter of Paul's in the New Testament and is almost entirely personal rather than doctrinal.

Paul was deeply concerned for Onesimus and wanted him to right the wrong he had done his master. Therefore he sent him back to his former household with this letter asking that the young man be received and forgiven by his owner.

The opening three verses contain a salutation to Philemon, to several close associates, and to "the church in (his) house, . . ." The next four verses express Paul's thanksgiving, prayer, comfort, and commendation of the fellowship. In verses eight through twenty Paul asks for several favors, which include the acceptance and forgiveness of Onesimus, and a request that a guest room be prepared for himself in anticipation of a visit. He concludes this brief epistle with greetings from his fellow workers and his customary benediction: "The grace of the Lord Jesus Christ be with your spirit" (1:25).

Message

This is one of the finest treatises on forgiveness found in the Bible. It contains all the ingredients that make up the spiritual fulfillment of this experience. Beginning with the offense, we move on to the intercession; are faced with compassion; are inspired by substitutionary sacrifice; receive restoration to spiritual affection; and at last are born into a new relationship.

Paul saw Onesimus as one who had found a new master in Christ thus entitling him to be one with all other brothers in the faith. Though Paul did not lift his voice against slavery, he did express a spiritual evaluation of life that made such a practice untenable.

Author—St. Paul

See page 207

Date

This letter was probably written between the years A.D. 56 or 57 to A.D. 60 or 61.

THE LETTER TO THE HEBREWS

THIS book proposes to show that the revelation of God in Christ is superior to the revelation of God in the law, which is fulfilled in Christ.

Content

The first four chapters point up the superiority of Christ as a messenger from God, his very son. Then follows proof of his qualifications: above the angels, more important than Moses, and superior to Joshua and the Levitical high priest. Interspersed with such evidences of Christ's superiority are doctrinal treatments of the incarnation and the dangers of unbelief and disobedience.

In the early part of the fifth chapter and on through the ninth, comparisons cease between the Old Testament leaders and Christ, and we find the Messiah to be the author of salvation and the source of a better covenant. The problem of apostasy is mentioned and the effectiveness of Christ's sacrifice propounded.

Jesus is the living high priest in the likeness of Melchizedak, "who has become a priest, not according to a legal requirement concerning bodily descent but by the power of an indestructible life" (7:16). But Christ, unlike other priests, was confirmed by an oath of God: "This makes Jesus the surety of a better covenant" (7:22).

The next section, chapters ten, eleven, and twelve, shows the superior nature of Christ's sacrifice and his way for man, as over against the lesser sacrifices and the law. "For it is impossible that the blood of bulls and goats should take away sins" (10:4). Then follows a warning of the danger in rejecting the sacrifice of the New Covenant.

It very naturally follows that faith is the basic ingredient in man's salvation, such faith being exemplified in the history of the Jewish people and their leaders as found in the Old Covenant ("Testament"). The entire eleventh chapter is given to this exposition.

The twelfth chapter is a forthright challenge to accept Christ and by faith inherit the promises of old, a faith not shaken or disturbed: "Therefore let us be grateful for receiving a kingdom that cannot be shaken, . . . (12:28).

The conclusion in chapter thirteen is a sermon or homily on Christian attitudes and behavior, followed by personal salutations and requests for prayers.

Message

Here is a message of encouragement for those who are now distant from the time of the apostles and who are dependent for their faith upon the traditions and teachings passed on to them. The author is assuring them that in Christ and the New Covenant they will find sufficient strength for their difficulties—a faith that cannot be shaken.

All through this letter Christ is held up as the final mediator, the true high priest between God and man. In Him is certain salvation and the full pardon from sin. Hence, Christianity is the final and absolute religion and Christ the "high priest, one who is seated at the right hand of the throne of the Majesty in heaven, a minister in the sanctuary and the true tent which is set up not by man but by the Lord" (8:1-2).

Author

At one time this book was attributed to Paul, but this theory is now generally abandoned. The style, the content, particularly the theology, as well as other evidences support the idea of another writer. The earliest evidence does not attribute it to Paul, and all centuries have had strong doubters of his authorship.

Some have attributed the book to such Early Church leaders as Barnabas and Timothy. The author is unknown, and it appears likely that he will remain so.

Yet this should be said: Here is the best written of all the New Testament books. The Greek is the purest and the writing the most refined. Furthermore, the author showed a profound understanding of all the strands of his heritage—Jewish, Gentile, and Christian—and he displays the skills of both scholar and artist in weaving them together to the praise of Jesus Christ, his Lord.

Date

In the absence of external evidence, support of a possible date must be found within the book itself. It was addressed to second-generation Christians many of whose former leaders had died, although Timothy undoubtedly was living and freed from prison. With these facts in mind, the book could have been written as early as A.D. 68 or 70.

THE LETTER OF JAMES

THIS Letter, like 1 and 11 Peter, 1 John and Jude, is known as a General Epistle or Catholic Epistle because it is directed to Christians at large, rather than to individual churches.

The Epistle is in the nature of a tract addressed "to the twelve tribes in dispersion" (1:1).

Content

The five chapters can be roughly outlined as follows:

The opening verse is a salutation. Then follows a statement setting forth the nature of true religion when faced with temptation, and those essential qualities of moral stability which come from above, from God himself. Out of such a faith man finds power to act constructively toward others as well as to persevere in righteous living.

In the second chapter and the first twelve verses of the third, we are instructed in the basic qualities of Christian brotherhood, which includes the avoidance of discrimination based upon wealth or prestige and the duty to activate one's faith by good works; "Show me your faith apart from works and I by my work will show you my faith" (2:18). It also means that a true believer shall be careful in judging and shall bridle his tongue.

James now writes of true wisdom (3:13-5:18), first defining it as of spiritual derivation, being "pure, then peaceable, gentle, open to reason, full of mercy and good fruits, without uncertainty or insincerity" (3:17). Having established the meaning, he now goes on to write of wisdom in matters involving the church people in legal relationships, and in the activities of traders and profiteers. Even labor problems are treated, strongly condemning the exploiter. Then follows an exhortation to all, that they be patient, "for the coming of the Lord is at hand" (5:8).

The twelfth verse of Chapter Five stands out alone: It advises the use of plain language, "yes" or "no."

The Apostle in the next few passages commends the wisdom of patience even in the face of affliction.

The conclusion, stated in the closing two verses, is generalized advice regarding the treatment of those who have wandered into sin and error.

Message

James writes in such a practical manner as to make the message obvious in the "Content" itself. In this sense, the book is not unlike the book of Proverbs. He makes clear the ethical application of Christian truth in the work-a-day world. Christian behavior is more significant than faith, which stands in contrast with the Pauline emphasis on justification by faith.

Author

There is very little specific information about James other than his claim to "be a servant of God, and of the Lord Jesus Christ" (1:1). Traditionally, many scholars have considered him a brother of Jesus and the "bishop" of Jerusalem. On the other hand, there are a number of reasons why a later and different James might have written this letter.

Could a Jew of his background have written such competent Greek? Then, too, the possibility of the letter being written at a later date, as proposed by some, would exclude the brother of the Lord, who probably died A.D. 60-62. If his identity as a brother of Jesus is eliminated, then the author remains completely unknown.

Date

There is evidence to support an early date for the letter of James, perhaps as early as A.D. 45. The Jerusalem Council is not mentioned (A.D. 51) which suggests this early time. Neither is there mention made of the law so strongly championed by James, the brother of Jesus (Acts 15:13-21). On the other hand the denunciation of wealth as found in this letter was not common to an earlier period of the Church. This fact could indicate an unknown writer of a later date, perhaps as late as A.D. 90. Even Origen, a third-century Christian scholar, expressed his doubts when he spoke of this letter as the "so-called Epistle of James." All this permits a wide latitude in dating this letter.

THE FIRST LETTER OF PETER

THE Roman government, though totalitarian, was very tolerant of the many religious and ethnic groups that existed in the Empire. This tolerance was particularly true when a religious sect was basically interested in spiritual matters. The Book of Acts directly and indirectly indicates this kind of tolerance.

But by A.D. 60, the Christian Church, no longer a Jewish sect, was beginning to feel the antagonism and the repressive measures of Roman officials who were suspicious of the strange talk of a coming judgment and of the overthrow of the world. We might say that Paul's death dates the beginning of organized Roman hostility and persecution.

First Peter is a response to this rising oppression, especially as it concerns the churches of northern Asia Minor.

Content

The letter opens with a salutation addressed to Christians, probably of Jewish background, who were "exiles of the dispersion in Pontus, Galatia, Capadocia, Asia, and Bithnyia." Also in this opening paragraph, Peter identifies himself as an apostle of Jesus Christ.

The remainder of the first chapter through ten verses in the second strongly emphasizes the hope of man in the resurrection of Christ. Peter sees this hope in both personal and social terms. He writes of faith in spite of persecution and admonishes his readers to live lives capable of receiving this hope: " 'All flesh is like grass . . . but the word of the Lord abides forever.' That word is the good news which was preached to you" (1:24-25).

The next division, Chapters 2:10 to 4:6, consists of instructions for the conduct of the redeemed. These exhortations cover the basic principles of Christian behavior regarding the world, the state, other individuals, and members of one's household. He concludes this portion by encouraging them to be brave in the face of persecution. "For this is why the gospel was preached even to the dead, that though judged in the flesh like men, they might live in the spirit like God" (4:6).

From this point on to the end of the fourth chapter, Peter writes of "the fiery ordeal," stressing the importance of sharing in Christ's pain, wherein "his glory is revealed" (4:13).

The last chapter, other than the salutation, is given over to the duties of the elders in ministering to the suffering, counselling them that Christians should have patience, knowing that "the God of all grace, who has called (them) to his eternal glory in Christ, will himself restore, establish, and strengthen (them)" (5:10).

Purpose

This letter is to give courage and strength to Christians who are under pressure from the ridicule of the pagan and from persecution by the state. Peter wants them to exemplify their faith in Christ by finding in his suffering and resurrection sufficient hope for their trials.

No book in the New Testament gives a stronger witness to the spirit of Christ and the power of God than First Peter.

If it was the author's purpose to make the Gospel come alive, to make the suffering, death, and resurrection of Jesus a source of spiritual awakening, then he accomplishes it.

Author

The author of this epistle was Simon Peter, the outstanding disciple of Jesus. He was a Galilean fisherman who left his boat when called by Christ to become a fisher of men.

His given name was Simon. Jesus, however, nicknamed him Peter, which means rock. The Master saw in him a firm and dependable leader, this in spite of his impetuousness, his vacillation, and earlier instability. And Peter became the Rock that Jesus saw in him.

This natural leader contributed only two books to the canon of the New Testament, but his genius as an organizer and evangelist was indispensable to establishing the Church.

Date

There is strong evidence that Peter died in Rome. The early Fathers were convinced of this, and being within a few generations of Peter's time, could be correct in their belief. Such early scholars and Church Fathers as Clement of Rome, Ignatius, Dionysius, Irenaeus and Tertullian, to mention a few, were absolutely convinced that Peter was with Paul and succeeded him in Rome.

Modern scholars, sifting the available evidence, believe this letter could have been written from Rome shortly before A.D. 64, perhaps even earlier than A.D. 60, while Peter was on a brief visit to the Imperial City.

THE SECOND LETTER OF PETER

WHEREAS the author of First Peter gave courage and faith to the suffering, the author of Second Peter seeks to drive out error with truth. Knowledge is the key word in this book.

Content

Following the usual salutation we find the letter to be made up of briefly stated themes:

Chapter one points out the nature of divine truth and challenges the Christian to grow in the knowledge of the Lord Jesus Christ. Out of such truth comes the promise of salvation.

Chapter two deals with error and condemns and discloses false teachers. Man is lost when he abandons the knowledge of the Lord Jesus Christ; indeed, he is doubly hurt when he reverts to error, having once known the truth.

The last chapter can be broken into two sections. The first thirteen verses remind the reader of Christ's return without attempting to specify the time, "that with the Lord one day is as a thousand years . . ." (3:8). At the same time the author hastens to add, "But the day of the Lord will come like a thief, . . ." (3:10).

The remaining verses refer to the responsibilities of Christians to live pure lives, to know the "error of lawless men," and to "grow in the grace and knowledge of our Lord Jesus Christ" (3:18).

Purpose

There had been a decline in the belief in the second coming of Christ, the Parousia. This skepticism had grown progressively stronger as the result of heretical teaching, particularly that of the Gnostics. The writer of this letter seeks to restore and clarify this faith in the Lord's return.

But the writer also wanted the Scriptures to be properly interpreted and at the close of the first chapter penned one of the most impressive passages on this subject to be found in the New Testament: "First of all you must understand this, that no prophecy of scripture is a matter of one's own interpretation, because no prophecy ever came by the impulse of man, but men moved by the Holy Spirit spoke from God" (1:20-21).

Author

There is doubt concerning the authorship of this epistle even though the writer contends to be "Simon Peter, a servant and apostle of Jesus Christ . . ." (1:1). Even the Early Fathers fail to give it the traditional support assigned to the other New Testament books.

We must consider the sharp differences in vocabulary and style between the two letters. 11 Peter lacks the smooth, even flow of the Greek of the first letter. Yet others, ignoring this criticism, point to the contents which is doctrinally sound, and could well have been from the hand of Peter. Suffice it to say that the same historic doubts of the Early Church about this writer still exist today.

Date

There is no reference to the suffering of the church which could mean that the cruel persecution recently affecting Paul had for the moment passed away, and that the author no longer found it necessary to stress this problem. The letter could therefore have been written between the years A.D. 65 and 67.

THE THREE LETTERS OF JOHN

JOHN'S letters express a more practical theology and doctrine than his Gospel, which is especially true of the First Epistle. He intends that we see the everyday relationship of faith to life as found in history. In the Gospel he emphasizes the Jesus who is Christ in contrast to the emphasis in First John of the Christ who is Jesus.

This opening Letter is basically homiletical in form, purposing to give theological direction to the reader. In this sense, it is a pastoral epistle. John is anxious that our faith find application in Christian conduct and belief. His message is fellowship with God, with Christ and with our brothers. God becomes illumination, righteousness, and above all else, love. This faith is not sentimental, for the author sees God's love, along with his hatred of evil, as soundly rooted in discipline and obedience.

The other two letters are very brief and were for a long time considered to be of questionable canonical material. But by the fourth century they had become permanently acceptable to the Early Church.

The Second Epistle is addressed to an individual although it might well have been intended for a church. As in the previous letter, the emphasis is upon love, obedience and man's fellowship with God. To these virtues is added a warning concerning dangers and temptations confronting the ancient churches of Asia Minor. Indeed, such a message is still meaningful to the contemporary Christian of today.

The Third Epistle is lacking in doctrinal material being entirely concerned with advice for a man named Gaius. This letter is quite incidental, and its worth is to be gauged only when related to the other two Epistles.

This dependency of the Third Epistle upon the Second accounted for their always being found together. Jerome, A.D. 340-420, spoke of them as "twin sisters." John's Third Letter is a personal challenge to serve God through the brethren and to live an exemplary Christian life.

Author—St. John

See page 198

Date—About A.D. 100

See page 199

THE LETTER OF JUDE

THIS brief letter frankly states the necessity of abiding by rigorous standards of doctrine and faith. He insists upon the lordship of Christ defending the faithful against the dangers of apostasy.

Content

After a brief salutation Jude states bluntly the purpose of his note, which is to exhort them to be true to their faith and to be wary of those who excuse their immorality because God's forgiveness is so readily available, "ungodly persons who pervert the grace of our God into licentiousness and deny our only Master and Lord, Jesus Christ" (1:4).

From the fifth through the sixteenth verse there is a strong arraignment of apostasy, wherein the author specifies historic precedents of God's punishment of disobedience, such as Israel in the wilderness, the rebellious angels, and the burned cities of Sodom and Gomorrah. There are few passages in the Bible with such a vivid condemnation of error and disbelief.

The last section, verses seventeen through twenty-three, expound the hope and responsibility of Christians. The reader is reminded of apostolic teachings regarding "scoffers," "worldly people, devoid of the Spirit" (1:19), and is asked to wait upon the Lord as well as seek to save some who doubt.

The last two verses are among the best known and most quoted passages of the New Testament—a doxology and benediction.

Purpose

Jude is anxiously and firmly attacking those destructive forces affecting his Christian brethren. These foes had surreptitiously entered their ranks, falsely using God's grace as a reason for lascivious behavior. But his letter is more than a condemnation, for he concludes with a forthright appeal and challenge to keep the faith and rescue others from the apostasy which surrounds them.

Author

Jude traditionally has been identified as a brother of James and Jesus. Many scholars, however, say he was a brother of a later James, reminding us that the author does not claim apostolic status.

Date

The fact that Jude looks back upon the Apostolic Age indicates that he may have written his letter as late as A.D. 90. However there are those who think that Jude's epistle, having much in common with Peter's writings, could have been penned as early as A.D. 67 or 68.

THE REVELATION TO JOHN

THE book of Revelation is one of many such apocalyptic writings known to the Early Church. This particular literary style flourished for several centuries and then completely vanished as a mode of expression. The classic example of such writing in the Old Testament is the Book of Daniel.

Through the centuries Christians have debated the meaning, worth and purpose of the book. No other New Testament writing has caused so much controversy and created as much questionable dogmatism.

One group contends it is an allegorical picture of the Church's struggle with the Roman Empire. Others believe it prophesies and reveals the second coming of Jesus and the end of the world. A third body of believers sees it as a panorama of the Church from the beginning to the end of time, when Christ and His Church will triumph over the forces of evil. A fourth group sees the author disclosing in symbolic language the great principles of Divine Government. Of one thing we are certain, the language and symbolism were undoubtedly meaningful to the people of the first century, but have long since lost their potent significance as a way of expression, with the consequent loss of a full understanding of the author's meaning. It is therefore dangerous to speculate too freely concerning the symbols and hidden meanings.

The Book of Revelation was not at first universally accepted as of canonical status. Indeed, no less a scholar than Jerome questioned its validity, insisting that it be kept "under discussion" rather than be fully accepted. Yet as early as A.D. 150 it had become an important text for the Church, being credited to the Apostle John. As time went on, scholars in both the East and the West included it in the New Testament canon in spite of Jerome's concern as to its importance. Though it finally became a definite part of the Christian canon, it has always been given a lesser place among the other books of the New Testament. This evaluation is as true today as it was in Jerome's time.

The debate still goes on regarding authorship, whether John the Apostle, John the Presbyter or some other John was the writer. Much of this discussion in modern times centers around difference in style and emphasis as compared with the other Johannine books. But for our purpose, the significance of the writings need not be conditioned by this scholarly debate.

Content

The opening three verses are introductory, stating the purpose of the author which is to predict the nature of "things to come." It is a revelation of the course and destiny of the Church.

The first three chapters restrict themselves to conditions in John's time and are particularly concerned with what he calls the seven churches of Asia.

Chapters four through twenty-two comprise the last or second division of the book and prophetically cover the future unto the end, "Things which shall be hereafter" (4:1).

Most authorities agree with the following analysis of the contents of Revelation:

DIVISION I:

1. Introduction—Chapter 1
2. The Spirit Speaks to the Seven Churches—Chapters 2, 3

DIVISION II:

3. The Time of Conflict and Distress—Chapters 4-7
4. The Final Messianic Struggle—Chapters 8-14
5. The Messianic Victory—Chapters 15-20
6. The Messianic Kingdom—Chapters 21-22:5
7. Epilogue—Chapter 22:6-21

Let us now focus our attention upon the purpose and insight of this book of revelation and mystery.

Message

In spite of all the varied interpretations of the Book of Revelation, it still remains a significant and valuable religious text, permeated by the spirit of worship. In it we find the manifestation of God as seen in Christ, entering the world to redeem man from the slavery of sin, and the church struggling to serve and witness under persecution. God's grace finds ultimate expression in the Person of Christ, who enters the course of history and determines the ultimate victory of good over exil. Thus is established the Messianic Kingdom.

Beyond and even within the apocalyptic figurations of the book we discover the highest ideals of Christian personality, the victory of righteousness over public evils, and a God of love who is forever just.

Perhaps we should briefly consider the message to the Seven Churches which is so appropriate for our own time.

THE LETTER TO THE CHURCH IN EPHESUS (2:1-7)

The congregation had withstood false prophets but were now growing apathetic in their faith. They were lukewarm and half-hearted Christians. Thus was Christ hurt by their indifference.

THE LETTER TO THE CHURCH IN SMYRNA (2:8-11)

Here is a suffering church in need of encouragement. Poor people make up its membership, and though lacking in worldly prestige, the Christians of Smyrna are found to be rich in faith (2:9). No matter how persecuted they might be, they would in Christ, live forevermore.

THE LETTER TO THE CHURCH IN PERGAMUM (2:12-17)

This church was faithful to Christ even in the face of martyrdom (2:13) but at the same time permitted false teachings within its ranks. This led to the members tolerating heathen immoralities. The church is warned of the Lord's displeasure and the inevitable consequences of such spiritual vacillation.

THE LETTER TO THE CHURCH IN THYATIRA (2:18-29)

The Church was growing spiritually but endangering its life by a willingness to compromise. There was too much condoning of false teachings and especially a tragic willingness of the pastors to accept as a fellow leader a pagan woman called "Jezebel." She was not only introducing, but insisting that it was the right of Christians, to practice many pagan and licentious acts. This displeased the Lord, the "Son of God, with eyes like fire and feet like brass" (2:18).

THE LETTER TO THE CHURCH IN SARDIS (3:1-6)

The Church in Sardis was spiritually dead. Only the name was left. A few faithful ones would be saved, but the church would be erased (3:5), blotted from Heaven's roll.

THE LETTER TO THE CHURCH IN PHILADELPHIA (3:7-13)

The Christians of this ancient city were faithful followers of Christ, living their religion without officiously meddling in the affairs of the community. They were satisfied to bear witness of Christ in a pagan and corrupt environment. The Lord loved this church and did not rebuke it.

THE LETTER TO THE CHURCH IN LAODICEA (3:14-22)

The Lord strongly disapproved of this church's self-satisfaction and downright indifference. In fact, Christ was outside the door trying to gain admittance to his Church in Laodicea (3:20).

This concluding book of the New Testament was in reality a "tract for the times," addressed to the Christian underground during the persecution of the Church by Emperor Domitian. The early Christians understood the symbolism and found solace and strength in its message. We, too, can discover meaning for our time by seeking, beyond the symbolism, the truth the author intended for his contemporaries. In the Book of Revelation the Kingdom of Christ transfigures history, assuring us that God's redemptive love will ultimately triumph. Christ, the Lamb of God, slain for a sinful world, will prevail over the forces of evil that have corrupted history. Thus shall be born a new man in Christ as was originally planned in the first Creation.

Author

The only clue we have to the authorship of Revelation is to be found in the book itself. The writer refers to himself as John (1:4,9).

The style and content identify the book as written by one

man, and by a man other than the author of the Gospel and Letters of John. Whoever he was, he had been banished from Rome to the Island of Patmos where he penned the "Apocalypse" (Revelation).

John of Patmos is perhaps the most descriptive name we can give this prophet and theologian who nowhere claims to be an Apostle or to have known Jesus personally. Yet he writes as one inspired by Christ through the voice of the Holy Spirit.

Date

It is quite evident that the author, having been banished to the Island of Patmos, is anxious to strengthen the Christian communities of Asia Minor against the continuing persecution of Domitian. Hence, the book was probably written sometime during the last years of Emperor Domitian's reign, A.D. 81-96.

OLD TESTAMENT BIBLIOGRAPHY

THE BIBLE

DODD, C. H. The Authority of the Bible, New York: Harper & Bros., 1929.

ROWLEY, H. H. The Relevance of the Bible. New York: The Macmillan Co., 1944.

THE CANON

BUDDE, KARL. Article, "Canon Old Testament," in T. K. Cheyne, ed., Encyclopedia Biblica. New York: The Macmillan Co., 1899. Vol. I. pp. 649-74.

MARGOLIS, M. L. The Hebrew Scriptures in the Making. Philadelphia: Jewish Publication Society of America, 1922.

STRACK, H. L. Article, "Canon of Scripture," in S. M. Jackson, ed., The New Schaff-Herzog Encyclopedia, New York: Funk & Wagnalls, 1908. Vol. II, pp. 388-93.

ZEITLIN, S. An Historical Study of the Canonization of the Hebrew Scriptures. Philadelphia: Jewish Publication Society of America, 1933.

THE APOCRYPHAL BOOKS AND THE OLD TESTAMENT CANON

CHARLES, R. H. Religious Development Between the Old and New Testaments, New York: Henry Holt, 1914.

GOODSPEED, EDGAR J. The Apocrypha: An American Translation. Chicago: University of Chicago Press, 1938.

OESTERLEY, W.O.E. An Introduction to the Books of the Apocrypha. New York: The Macmillan Co., 1937.

TORREY, C. C. The Apocryphal Literature: A Brief Introduction. New Haven: Yale University Press, 1945.

BIBLE CRITICISM

COPPENS, JOSEPH. The Old Testament and the Critics, tr. Edward A. Ryan and Edward W. Tribbe. Paterson, N.J.: St. Anthony Guild Press. 1942.

FARAR, FREDERIC WILLIAM. History of Interpretation. New York: E. P. Dutton & Co., 1886.

ROWLEY, H. H., ed. The Old Testament and Modern Study. Oxford: Clarendon Press, 1951.

WILLOUGHBY, HAROLD R., ed. The Study of the Bible Today and Tomorrow. Chicago: University of Chicago Press, 1947.

(TORAH) THE PENTATEUCH

BISSELL, E. E. The Pentateuch. New York, 1885

CARPENTER, J. E. and G. HARFORD, The Composition of the Hexateuch. London and New York, 1904.

GENESIS

DRIVER, S. R. The Book of Genesis ("Westminster Commentaries"). 15th ed. London: Methuen & Co., 1948.

GORDON, ALEXANDER R. The Early Tradition of Genesis, Edinburgh: T. & T. Clark, 1907.

SKINNER, JOHN A Critical and Exegetical Commentary on Genesis ("International Critical Commentary"). Rev. ed. New York Charles Scribner's Sons, 1925.

EXODUS

DRIVER, S. R. The Book of Exodus ("The Cambridge Bible"). Cambridge: Cambridge University Press, 1911.

MEEK, THEOPHILE J. Hebrew Origins. Rev. ed. New York: Harper & Bros., 1950.

LEVITICUS

CHAPMAN, A. T., and STREANE, A. W. The Book of Leviticus ("The Cambridge Bible"). Cambridge: Cambridge University Press. 1914.

KELLOGG, S. H. The Book of Leviticus ("The Expositor's Bible"). New York: A. C. Armstrong & Son, 1891.

NUMBERS

BINNS, L. ELLIOTT. The Book of Numbers ("Westminster Commentaries"). London: Methuen & Co., 1927.

GRAY, GEORGE BUCHANON. A Critical and Exegetical Commentary of Numbers ("International Critical Commentary"). New York: Charles Scribner's Sons, 1903.

HASTINGS, JAMES, ed. Dictionary of the Bible. New York: Charles Scribner's Sons, 1898-1904.

DEUTERONOMY

ROBINSON, H. WHEELER Deuteronomy and Joshua ("The New-Century Bible"). New York: Oxford University Press, 1908.

SMITH, GEOGRE ADAM. The Book of Deuteronomy ("The Cambridge Bible"). Cambridge: Cambridge University Press, 1918.

WELCH, ADAM C. The Code of Deuteronomy. London: James Clarke & Co., 1924.

JOSHUA

OOKE, G. A. The Book of Joshua ("The Cambridge Bible"). Cambridge: University Press, 1918.

ROBINSON, H. WHEELER. Deuteronomy and Joshua ("The New Century Bible"). New York: Oxford University Press, 1908.

ROWLEY, H. H. From Joseph to Joshua. London Oxford University Press, 1950.

JUDGES

COOKE, G. A. The Book of Judges ("The Cambridge Bible"). Cambridge: Cambridge University Press, 1913.

MOORE, G. F. A Critical and Exegetical Commentary on Judges ("International Critical Commentary"). New York: Charles Scribner's Sons, 1895.

THATCHER, G. W. Judges and Ruth ("The New Century Bible"). New York: Oxford University Press, 1904.

SAMUEL 1 and 2

PFEIFFER, R. H. Introduction to the Old Testament. New York: Harper & Bros. 1941.

SMITH, HENRY PRESERVED. A Critical and Exegetical Commentary on the Books of Samuel ("International Critical Commentary"). New York: Charles Scribner's Sons, 1899.

KINGS 1 and 2

BARNES, W. E. The First Book of the Kings ("The Cambridge Bible"). Cambridge: Cambridge University Press, 1911.

MONTGOMERY, J. A. and GEHMAN, H. S. A Critical and Exegetical Commentary on the Books of Kings ("International Critical Commentary"). Edinburgh: T. & T. Clark, 1951.

SKINNER, JOHN. Kings ("The New-Century Bible"). New York: Oxford University Press, 1904.

NEVIIM—THE PROPHETS

LODS, ADOLPHE. The Prophets and the Rise of Judaism, tr. S. H. Hooke. New York: E. P. Dutton & Co., 1937.

ROBINSON, THEODORE H. Prophecy and the Prophets in Ancient Israel. New York: Charles Scribner's Sons, 1923.

SKINNER, JOHN. Prophecy and Religion. Cambridge: The University Press, 1922.

SMITH, J. M. P. The Prophets and Their Times. 2nd rev. William A. Irwin. Chicago: University of Chicago Press, 1941.

ISAIAH

BOX, G. H. The Book of Isaiah. London: Isaac Pitman & Sons, 1908.

GRAY, GEORGE BUCHANAN. A Critical and Exegetical Commentary on the Book of Isaiah I-XXXI ("International Critical Commentary). New York: Charles Scribner's Sons, 1912 Vol. I.

SKINNER, JOHN. The Book of the Prophet Isaiah ("The Cambridge University Press, 1915).

SMITH, GEORGE ADAM. The Book of Isaiah. New and rev. ed. London: Hodder & Stoughton, 1927.

JEREMIAH

PEAKE, A. S., ed. Jeremiah and Lamentations ("The New-Century Bible"). Edinburgh: T. C. & E. C. Jack, 1910-12.

SKINNER, JOHN. Prophecy and Religion. Cambridge: Cambridge University Press, 1922.

SMITH, GEORGE ADAM. Jeremiah. 4th ed. Garden City: Doubleday, Doran & Co., 1929.

EZEKIEL

COOKE, G. A. A Criitical and Exegetical Commentary on the Book of Ezekiel ("International Critical Commentary"). New York: Charles Scribner's Sons, 1937.

HARFORD, JOHN BATTERSBY. Studies in the Book of Ezekiel. Cambridge: Cambridge University Press, 1935.

TORREY, C. C. Pseudo-Ezekiel and the Original Prophecy. New Haven: Yale University Press. 1930.

HOSEA

HARPER, WILLIAM R. A Critical and Exegetical Commentary on Amos and Hosea ("International Critical Commentary"). New York: Charles Scribner's Sons. 1910.

ROBINSON, H. WHEELER. Two Hebrew Prophets, London: Lutterworth Press, 1948.

SMITH, GEORGE ADAM. The Book of the Twelve Prophets. Rev. ed. New York: Harper & Bros., 1928, Vol. I.

JOEL

CALKINS, RAYMOND. The Modern Message of the Minor Prophets. New York: Harper & Bros., 1947.

SMITH, GEORGE ADAM. The Book of the Twelve Prophets. Rev. ed. New York: Harper & Bros., 1928.

WADE, G. W. The Books of the Prophets, Micah, Obadiah, Joel, and Jonah ("Westminster Commentaries"). London: Methuen & Co., 1925.

AMOS

SMITH, GEORGE ADAM. The Book of the Twelve Prophets. Rev. ed. New York: Harper & Bros., 1940. Vol. I.

WOLFE, ROLLAND E. Meet Amos and Hosea. New York: Harper & Bros., 1945.

OBADIAH

BREWER, JULIUS A. A Critical and Exegetical Commentary on Obadiah and Joel ("International Critical Commentary"). New York: Charles Scribner's Sons, 1911.

CALKINS, RAYMOND. The Modern Message of the Minor Prophets. New York: Harper & Bros., 1947.

JONAH

SMITH, GEORGE ADAM. The Book of the Twelve Prophets. Rev. ed. New York: Harper & Bros., 1928.
WADE, G. W. The Books of the Prophets ("Westminster Commentaries"). London: Methuen & Co., 1925.

MICAH

TAIT, ARTHUR J. The Prophecy of Micah. New York: Charles Scribner's Sons, 1917.

NAHUM

DAVIDSON, A. B. The Books of Nahum, Habakkuk and Zephaniah ("Cambridge Bible"). Cambridge: Cambridge University Press, 1920.
DRIVER, S. R., ed. The Minor Prophets ("New Century Bible"). New York: Oxford University Press, 1906. Vol. II.
SMITH, GEORGE ADAM. The Book of the Twelve Prophets. Rev. ed. New York: Harper & Bros., 1928 Vol. II.

HABAKKUK

DAVIDSON, A. B. The Books of Nahum, Habakkuk and Zephaniah ("Cambridge Bible"). Cambridge: Cambridge University Press, 1920.
SMITH, GEORGE ADAM. The Book of the Twelve Prophets. Rev. ed. New York: Harper & Bros., 1928 Vol. II.

ZEPHANIAH

DRIVER, S. R., ed. The Minor Prophets ("New Century Bible"). New York: Oxford University Press, 1906. Vol. II.
SMITH, GEORGE ADAM. The Book of the Twelve Prophets. Rev. ed. New York: Harper & Bros., 1928. Vol. II.

HAGGAI

BARNES, W. E. Haggai and Zechariah ("Cambridge Bible"). Cambridge: Cambridge University Press, 1917.
DRIVER, S. R., ed. The Minor Prophets ("New Century Bible"). New York: Oxford University Press, 1906. Vol. II.

ZECHARIAH

BARNES, W. E. Haggai and Zechariah ("Cambridge Bible"). Cambridge: Cambridge University Press, 1917.
DRIVER, S. R., ed. The Minor Prophets ("New Century Bible"). New York: Oxford University Press, 1906. Vol. II.

MALACHI

SMITH, GEORGE ADAM. The Book of the Twelve Prophets. Rev. ed. New York: Harper & Bros., 1928. Vol. II.

KETHUBIM (Wisdom Writings)

DRIVER, S. R., and GRAY, G. B. A Critical and Exegetical Commentary on the Book of Job ("International Critical Commentary"). New York: Charles Scribner's Sons, 1921.

MACDONALD, D. B. The Hebrew Philosophical Genius. Princeton: Princeton University Press, 1936.

RANKIN, O. S. Israel's Wisdom Literature. Edinburgh: T. & T. Clark, 1936.

RANSTON, HARRY. The Old Testament Wisdom Books and Their Teaching. London: Epworth Press, 1930.

THE PSALMS

JAMES, FLEMING. Thirty Psalmists, New York: G. P. Putnam's Sons, 1938.

KIRKPATRICK, A. F. The Book of Psalms ("Cambridge Bible"). Cambridge: Cambridge University Press, 1902.

LESLIE, ELMER. The Psalms. New York and Nashville: Abingdon-Cokesbury Press, 1949.

PROVERBS

COHEN, ABRAHAM, Proverbs. Hindhead, Surrey: Soncino Press, 1945.

MARTIN, G. C. Proverbs, Ecclesiastes and Song of Songs ("The New-Century Bible"). New York: Oxford University Press, 1908.

OESTERLEY, W. O. E. The Book of Proverbs ("Westminster Commentaries"). London: Methuen & Co., 1929.

PEROWNE, T. T. The Proverbs ("The Cambridge Bible"). Cambridge: Cambridge University Press, 1916.

JOB

DRIVER, S. R., and GRAY, G. B. A Critical and Exegetical Commentary on the Book of Job ("International Critical Commentary"). New York: Charles Scribner's Sons, 1921.

PEAKE, A. S. Job ("The Century Bible"). London: T. C. & E. C. Jack, 1904.

WATSON, ROBERT ADDISON. The Book of Job ("The Expositor's Bible"). New York: A. C. Armstrong & Son. 1899.

SONG OF SONGS

BETTAN, ISRAEL, The Five Scrolls. Cincinnati: Union of American Hebrew Conrgegations, 1950.

CANNON, W. W. The Song of Songs. Cambridge: Cambridge University Press, 1913.

GORDIS, ROBERT. The Song of Songs: A Study, Modern Translations and Commentary. New York: Jewish Theological Seminary of America, 1954.

RUTH

COOK, G. A. The Book of Ruth ("The Cambridge Bible"). Cambridge: Cambridge University Press, 1913.

MACDONALD, D. B. The Hebrew Literary Genius. Princeton: Princeton Press. 1933. Pp. 121-23.

SLOTKI, J. R. "Ruth" in The Five Megilloth, ed. Abraham Cohen. Hindhead, England: Soncino Press, 1946.

WATSON, ROBERT ADDISON. Judges and Ruth ("Expositor's Bible"). New York: A. C. Armstrong & Sons, 1899.

LAMENTATIONS

BETTAN, ISRAEL, The Five Scrolls. Cincinnati: Union of American Hebrew Conrgegations, 1950.

STREANE, A. W. The Book of the Prophet Jeremiah Together with the Lamentations ("Cambridge Bible"). Cambridge: Cambridge University Press, 1913.

ECCLESIASTES

BARTON G. A. The Book of Ecclesiastes ("International Critical Commentary"). New York: Charles Scribner's Sons, 1908.

GORDIS, ROBERT. The Wisdom of Ecclesiastes. New York: Behrman House 1945.

RANSTON, HARRY. Ecclesiastes and the Early Greek Wisdom Literature. London: Epworth Press, 1925.

ESTHER

PATON, L. B. A Critical and Exegetical Commentary on the Book of Esther ("International Critical Commentary"). New York: Charles Scribner's Sons, 1908.

PFEIFFER, R. H. Introduction to the Old Testament, New York: Harper & Bros., 1941. Pp: 732-42.

STREANE, A. W. Esther ("Cambridge Bible"). Cambridge: Cambridge University Press, 1907.

DANIEL

BEVAN, A. A. A Critical Commentary on the Book of Daniel. Cambridge: Cambridge University Press, 1892.

DRIVER, S. R. The Book of Daniel ("Cambridge Bible"). Cambridge: University Press, 1922.

GINSBERG, H. L. Studies in Daniel. New York: Jewish Theological Seminary of America, 1948.

EZRA and NEHEMIAH

BATTEN, L. W. A Critical and Exegetical Commentary on the Books of Ezra and Nehemiah ("International Critical Commentary") New York: Charles Scribner's Sons, 1913.

ROWLEY, H. H. The Servant of the Lord and Other Essays on the Old Testament. London: Lutterworth Press, 1952. Pp. 131-59.

CHRONICLES 1 and 2

CURTIS, EDWARD L., and MADSEN, ALBERT A. A Critical and Exegetical Commentary on the Books of Chronicles ("International Critical Commentary"). New York: Charles Scribner's Sons, 1910.

WELCH, ADAM C. The Work of the Chronicler, London: British Academy, 1939.

NEW TESTAMENT BIBLIOGRAPHY

MACGREGOR, GEDDES. The Making of the Bible. Philadelphia. New York: J. B. Lippincott Co., 1959.

RALL, HARRIS FRANKLIN. New Testament History. New York—Nashville: Abingdon Press, 1914.

TENNEY, MERRIL C. New Testament Survey, Rev. Ed. Grand Rapids: Wm. B. Eerdmans Publishing Co., 1961.

THE CANON OF THE NEW TESTAMENT

HOLDSWORTH, W. W. Gospel Origins. New York: Charles Scribner's Sons, 1913.

RIGGS, J.S. "The Canon of the New Testament" in the International Standard Bible Encyclopedia. Grand Rapids: Wm. B. Eerdmans Publishing Co., 1949.

SOUTER, ALEXANDER. The Text and Canon of the New Testament. New York: Charles Scribner's Sons, 1923.

THE GOSPELS

JACKSON, HENRY L. "The Present State of the Synoptic Problem" in the Cambridge Biblical Essays, H. B. Swete, Editor. London: MacMillan and Co., Ltd., 1909.

SCHWEITZER, ALBERT. The Quest of the Historical Jesus: A.C. Black, 1910.

SCOTT, ERNEST FINDLAY. The Validity of the Gospel Record. New York: Charles Scribner's Sons, 1938.

SCROGGIE, W. GRAHAM. A Guide to the Gospels. London: Pickering and Inglis, 1948.

TAYLOR, VINCENT. The Formulation of the Gospel Tradition. New York: The Macmillan Co., 1935.

WESTCOTT, B. F. Introduction to the Study of the Gospel. London: MacMillan and Co., Ltd., 1888.

ST. MATTHEW

BROADUS, JOHN A. Commentary on the Gospel of Matthew in the American Commentary. Philadelphia: American Baptist Publication Society, 1886.

MC NEILE, ALAN HUGH. The Gospel According to St. Matthew, London: The MacMillan Co., 1915.

SMITH, B.T.D. The Gospel According to Matthew. Cambridge: Cambridge University Press, 1927.

ST. MARK

BRANSCOMB, B. HARVIE. The Gospel of Mark. New York: Harper & Brothers, 1937.

MORGAN, G. CAMPBELL. The Gospel According to Mark. New York: Fleming H. Revell Co., 1927.

RAWLINSON, A. E. J. St. Mark. London: Methuen & Co., 1931.

ST. LUKE

EASTON, BURTON SCOTT. The Gospel According to St. Luke. New York: Charles Scribner's Sons, 1926.

HARNACK, ADOLPH. Luke the Physician. New York: G. P. Putnam's Son's, 1902.

I UCE, H. K. The Gospel According to St. Luke: Cambridge University Press, 1933

ST. JOHN

HOWARD, W.F. Edited by A. W. Harrison, Christianity According to St. John. London: Duckworth, 1943.

SCOTT, ERNEST FINDLEY. The Fourth Gospel, Its Purpose and Theology. Edinburgh: T. & T. Clark, 1908.

SMART, W. A. The Spiritual Gospel. New York. Nashville: Abington Cokesbury Press, 1945.

TENNEY, MERRILL C. John: The Gospel of Belief. Grand Rapids: Wm. B. Eerdmans Publishing Co., 1951.

THE LETTERS OF PAUL

ROMANS

BARRETT, C. K. A Commentary on the Epistle to the Romans. New York: Harper, 1957.

FORRESTER, E. J. A Righteousness of God for Unrighteous Men. New York: G. H. Doran Co., 1926.

I CORINTHIANS

MOFFATT, J. Moffatt New Testament Commentary: The First Epistle of Paul to the Corinthians. New York: Harper, 1938.

ROBERTSON, A. and A. PLUMMER. International Critical Commentary: The First Epistle of Paul to the Corinthians. New York: Scribner, 1911.

II CORINTHIANS

MENZIES, ALLEN. The Second Epistle of the Apostle Paul to the Corinthians London: MacMillan & Co., Ltd., 1912.

STRACHAN, R. H. Moffatt New Testament Commentary: The Second Epistle of Paul to the Corinthians, New York: Harper, 1935.

GALATIANS

BURTON, E. D. International Critical Commentary: The Epistle to the Galatians. New York: Scribner, 1920.

EPHESIANS

BROWN, JOHN. An Exposition of the Epistle to the Galatians. Evansville, Ind.: The Sovereign Grace Book Club, 1957.

ROBINSON, J. ARMITAGE. St. Paul's Epistle to the Ephesians. London: Macmillan, 1909.

PHILIPPIANS

MULLER, JAC. J. The Epistle of Paul to the Philippians and to Philemon, the New International Commentary on the New Testament. Grand Rapids: Wm. B. Eerdmans Publishing Co., 1955.

COLOSSIANS

JONES, MAURICE. The Epistle of St. Paul to the Colossians. London: Society for Promoting Christian Knowledge, 1923.

MOULE, C.F.D. The Epistle to the Colossians and to Philemon. Cambridge: Cambridge, 1957.

I AND II THESALONIANS

ELLICOTT, CHARLES J. Commentary on the Epistles of St. Paul to the Thesalonians. Grand Rapids: Zondervan Publishing House, 1957.

NEIL, W. Moffatt New Testament Commentary: The Epistles of Paul to the Thesalonians. New York: Harpers, 1950.

PLUMMER, ALFRED. A Commentary on St. Paul's Epistle to the Thesalonians. London: R. Scott, 1918.

THE PASTORAL EPISTLES
I AND II TIMOTHY AND JUDE

EATON, B. S. The Pastoral Epistles. New York: Scribner, 1947.

SIMPSON, E. K. The Pastoral Epistles. Grand Rapids: Wm. B. Eerdmans Publishing Co., 1954.

PHILEMON

MOULE, C. F. D. The Epistles to Colossians and to Philemon. Combridge: Cambridge, 1957.

HEBREWS

DAVIDSON, A. P. Hebrews. Edinburgh: T. and T. Clark, 1950.

MOFFATT, J. International Critical Commentary: The Epistle to the Hebrews. New York: Scribner, 1924.

MOULE, H.C.D. Messages from the Epistle to the Hebrews. London: Chas. J. Thynne & Jarvis, Ltd., 1930.

JAMES

ROPES, J. H. A. International Critical Commentary: The Epistle to James. New York: Scribner, 1916.

I PETER

BEARE, F. W. The First Epistle of Peter. New York: MacMillan, 1947.

SELWYN, E. G. The First Epistle of St. Peter. London: MacMillan, 1952.

II PETER

WAND, JOHN W. C. The General Epistles of St. Peter and Jude. London: Methuen & Co., 1934.

THE JOHANNINE EPISTLES

DODD, C. H. Moffatt New Testament Commentary: The Johannine Epistles. New York: Harper, 1946.

JUDE

See Pastoral Epistles.

REVELATION

KIDDLE, M. Moffatt New Testament Commentary: Revelation. New York: Harpers, 1940.

RAMSAY, WILLIAM. The Letters to the Seven Churches of Asia. New York: George H. Doran Co., 1905.